KINDERGARTEN TECHNOLOGY

32 LESSONS EVERY KINDERGARTNER CAN ACCOMPLISH ON A COMPUTER

FIFTH EDITION

Part One of Nine in the SL Technology Curriculum

© *2013 Structured Learning LLC*

Fifth Edition 2013
Part One of Structured Learning's nine-volume Technology Curriculum

Visit the companion site http://askatechteacher.com© for more tech resources

Your wiki number is K5-30-48. Use this to access free resources here

To receive free technology tips and websites, send an email to admin@structuredlearning.net with the message "Subscribe to Weekly Tips and Websites"

ISBN 0-9787800-0-0

Published in the United States of America by Structured Learning LLC

Introduction

The educational paradigm has changed. New guidelines (most recently, the National Board of Governors <u>Common Core Standards</u>) expect technology to *facilitate learning through collaboration, publishing, and transfer of knowledge*. Educators want students to use technology to *work together, share the products of their effort, and employ the skills learned in other parts of their lives*.

How do we as teachers facilitate collaboration-publishing-transfer of knowledge?

We do it with the Structured Learning Technology Curriculum as roadmap. Aligned with <u>Common Core State Standards*</u> and <u>National Educational Technology Standards,</u> and using a time-proven method honed in classrooms, students learn the technology that promotes literacy, critical thinking, problem-solving, and decision-making. The purpose is not to teach step-by-step computer skills (like adding borders, formatting a document, creating a blog). There are many fine books for that. What this curriculum does is guide you to providing the **right information at the right time**. Just as most children can't learn to read at two, or write at four, they shouldn't be required to place hands on home row in kindergarten or use the internet before they understand the risks and responsibilities. We make sure students get what they need at the right age. The end result is a phenomenal amount of learning in a short period of time.

Fifth Edition 2013
Part One of Structured Learning's Technology Curriculum

Visit the companion site http://askatechteacher.com© for more tech resources

Your wiki number is K5-30-48. Use this to access *free resources here*

To receive free technology tips and websites, send an email to admin@structuredlearning.net with the message "Subscribe to Weekly Tips and Websites"

If there are skills you as teacher don't know, visit our Help blog (<u>AskATechTeacher.wordpress.com</u>) and co-teaching <u>wikis:</u>

- <u>K-3rd grade — http://smaatechk-3.wikispaces.com/</u>
- <u>4th grade — http://smaatech-fourthgrade.wikispaces.com/</u>
- <u>5th grade — http://smaatech.wikispaces.com/</u>

…for free help (use wiki number on book face page for access—see inset). All are staffed by tech teachers ready to help you.

What's in the SL Technology Curriculum?

Here's what you'll find:

- *Experiential learning with real-world applications*
- *Inquiry-based projects, exercises and assignments*
- *Collaboration among students and teachers*

- *Opportunities for students to express and grow in their creativity*
- *International mindedness*

Here's a quick overview of what is included in this textbook:

- *Scope and Sequence of skills taught*
- *Step-by-step weekly lessons*
- *Monthly homework (3rd-5th only)*
- *Certificate of Completion for students*
- *Comprehensive list of websites to support learning*
- *Articles that address tech pedagogy*
- *Posters ready to print and hang on your walls*

Each lesson includes:

- *Common Core Standards**
- *ISTE Standards*
- *essential question*
- *big idea*
- *materials required*
- *vocabulary used*
- *problem solving for lesson*
- *time required to complete*
- *teacher preparation required*
- *steps to accomplish goals*
- *assessment strategies*
- *troubleshooting*
- *how to extend learning*
- *additional resources*
- *examples, grading rubrics*

Throughout the text are links to extend lessons, add enrichment, and/or provide flexibility in your teaching. No PDF? Google the website or contact our help sites.

Programs Used in these Textbooks

Programs used in this curriculum focus on skills that serve the fullness of a student's educational career. Free alternatives are noted where available:

General	K-2	3-8
Email	*Drawing program (or KidPix, TuxPaint)*	*Office (or Open Office, Google Docs)*
Google Earth	*Keyboard software or Free online site*	*MS Publisher*
Internet	*MS Office (or Open Office, Google Docs)*	*Adobe Photoshop (or Gimp)*
Web tools	*MS Publisher*	*Keyboard software or online tool*

What's New in the Fifth Edition?

A good curriculum is aligned with best practices. In technology, that means it must be updated every few years.

If you purchased SL's Fourth Edition, consider the following changes to technology in education since its 2011 publication:

- *Windows has updated their platform—twice*
- *iPads are the device of choice in the classroom*
- *Class Smartboards are more norm than abnorm(al)*
- *Technology in the classroom has changed from 'nice to have' to 'must have'*
- *1:1 has become a realistic goal*
- *Student research is as often done online as in the library*
- *Students spend as much time in a digital neighborhood as their home town*
- *Textbooks are considered resources rather than bibles*
- *Teachers who don't use technology are an endangered species*
- *Words like 'blended learning', 'authentic', 'transfer', 'evidence' are now integral to teaching*
- *Common Core Standards have swept like a firestorm through the education community, most timed to take effect after 2011*

In response, here are changes you'll find:

- *Each lesson notes which* **Common Core State Standard** *is addressed*
- *Each lesson reflects Common Core emphasis on comprehension, problem-solving, critical thinking,* **preparing students for career and college**
- *Students learn to* **understand the process**, *not just replicate a skill*
- *Lessons focus on* **transfer of knowledge**
- **Collaboration and sharing** *is often required*
- *Online support is offered through* **co-teaching wikis** *and a* **help blog**

Who Needs This Book

You are the Technology Specialist, Coordinator for Instructional Technology, IT Coordinator, Technology Facilitator, Curriculum Specialist, Technology Director, or tech teacher—tasked with finding the right project for a classroom. You have a limited budget, less software, and the drive to do it right no matter roadblocks.

Or you are the classroom teacher, a tech enthusiast with a goal this year—and this time you mean it—to integrate the wonders of technology into lessons. You've seen it work. Others in your PLN are doing it. And significantly, you want to comply with Common Core State Standards, ISTE, your state requirements, and/or IB guidelines that weave technology into the fabric of inquiry.

How do you reach your goal?

With this curriculum. It will give you confidence that your students are using technology for the blended learning required by state, national and international standards.

How to Use This Book

This technology curriculum is unlike others you've looked at. You are the guide for a class of learners. Lessons are student-centered and fluid, loosely presented as 4-6 week units, project- and skills-based. Depending upon age, units cover:

- *Word processing*
- *Desktop publishing*
- *Spreadsheets*
- *Presentations*

- *Internet use/Web-based tools*
- *Digital citizenship*
- *Google Earth*
- *Image editing*

A lesson is forty-five minutes. If there is a skill students don't get, spend additional time, especially when you see it come up a second or third time through the course of these textbooks. By the end of 8th grade, students have a well-rounded tech education that prepares them for college and/or career.

The table below tells you what's covered in which grade. Where units are taught multiple years, teaching reflects the Scope and Sequence, standards addressed, with increasingly less scaffolding and more student direction.

	Mouse Skills	Vocabulary - Hardware	Problem-solving	Windows and Basics	Keyboard and shortcuts	Word	Power Point	Publisher	Excel	Google Earth	Search/ Research	Graphics/ Visual Learning	Pro-gram'g	WWW	Robotics	Games	Dig Cit
K	☺	☺	☺	☺	☺					☺		☺		☺			☺
1	☺	☺	☺	☺	☺			☺	☺	☺		☺		☺			☺
2		☺	☺	☺	☺	☺	☺	☺	☺	☺		☺		☺			☺
3		☺	☺	☺	☺	☺	☺	☺	☺	☺	☺	☺		☺			☺
4		☺	☺		☺	☺	☺	☺	☺	☺	☺	☺		☺			☺
5		☺	☺		☺	☺		☺	☺	☺	☺	☺		☺			☺
6		☺	☺	☺	☺	☺	☺	☺	☺	☺	☺	☺		☺			☺
7		☺	☺	☺	☺				☺	☺	☺	☺	☺	☺	☺	☺	☺
8		☺	☺	☺	☺	☺			☺	☺	☺	☺	☺	☺	☺	☺	☺

Here are a few hints:

- Teach lessons in the order presented in the book (for grades K-5). Lessons introduce, reinforce, and circle back on the concept. Certain skills provide scaffolding for others so you want them solid before moving on. Resist the urge to mix up lessons, even if it seems your perfect time for a particular project comes earlier/later than placement in the book.
- We understand what happens when kids and technology collide—sparks. Sometimes you can't move on because students are too excited about what they're doing. No problem. Two solutions:

- Leave the line in front of uncompleted activities blank and return to it another week when you have time. You'll notice after using this curriculum for a few years that your students will get through more material, faster.
- Take an extra week. Most school years run 35-40 weeks. This book includes 32 lessons. This works also if you miss a class due to a holiday or field trip.

- Always use lesson vocabulary. Students gain authentic understanding of word use by your example.
- 'Teacher Preparation' often includes chatting with the class teacher. Why?

   - You want to tie your class conversations in with her/his inquiry.
   - You want to offer sponge websites for early-finishers that address her/his topics.

- Expect students to be risk takers. Don't rush to solve their problems. Ask them to think how it was done in the past. Focus on problems listed in the lesson, but embrace all that come your way.
- Throughout the year, circle back on lessons learned. It takes students five times seeing a skill to get it—

   - First: They barely hear you
   - Second: They try it
   - Third: They remember it
   - Fourth: They use it outside of class
   - Fifth: They tell a friend

Remind students throughout the year that they've learned the skills, are using them, and understand them. Check off skills in the Scope and Sequence additional times as you circle back on them.
- Join hundreds of teachers using the curriculum on our teaching wikis (links above). See how they handle issues. Ask questions. It's run by an educator who has used the curriculum for years. She'll help you. The only requirement is that you own this book.
- Need more help? Go to Ask a Tech Teacher©, our help blog (http://askatechteacher.com) run by a teacher using the curriculum.

Typical 45-minute Lesson

As you face a room full of eager faces, remember they learn best by doing.

> "Tell me and I'll forget.
> Show me and I may remember.
> Involve me and I'll understand."
> —Chinese Proverb (or Ben Franklin)

Don't take over the student's mouse and click for them or type in a web address when they need to learn that skill. Even if it takes longer, guide them to the answer so they know the path. If you've been doing this since kindergarten, you know it works. In fact, by the end of kindergarten, you saw remarkable results.

Here's how I run a class in the lab:

- Students start with 10 minutes of typing practice either on installed software or an online keyboarding program. Some days, youngers work instead on alphabet sites such as Bembo's Zoo or Starfall Letters (Google for websites)
- If it's the end of a grading period, I review which skills have been accomplished (see Scope and Sequence).
- If we are starting a new project, I review it, take questions and we start. If we are in the middle of one, students use the balance of class to work towards completion. I monitor activities, answer questions, help where needed. This portion of class is student-centered requiring critical thinking and problem-solving skills.
- As often as possible, I give younger students two weeks to finish a project—one to practice, one to save/export/print. This redundancy reinforces new skills and mitigates stress. If they are on week two, preparing to save/export/print, we start the day with the project and finish with typing to be sure students have as much time as possible to work.
- Students who complete the current project take advantage of age-appropriate 'sponge activities' from a topic that ties into class inquiry. I list websites on a class internet start page© (see inset for example of mine). Students know websites on this page can be used during sponge time.

Here are useful pieces to making your class tech productive and clear:

- *Textbook—the roadmap. Enough said.*
- *Class internet start page—enables you to provide a weekly update of what will happen in class complete with links and extensions. My students use this every time we're in class. It also provides a place to collect groups of links so you can direct students there quickly without recreating the list.*
- *Class wiki—provides detail on what happened during each class. You can also provide additional student and parent resources to enrich learning. Great for transparency with stakeholders and students who missed class.*

Copyrights

About the Authors

Structured Learning IT Team *is the premier provider of technology instruction books and ebooks to education professionals including curriculums, how-to guides, theme-based books, and a one-of-a-kind online helpline—all tools required to fulfill tech demands of the 21st century classroom. Materials are classroom-tested, teacher-approved with easy-to-understand directions supported by online materials, websites, blogs, and wikis. Whether you are a new teacher wanting to do it right or a veteran educator looking for updated materials,* **Structured Learning** *and its team of technology teachers is here to assist.*

Ask a Tech Teacher *is a group of technology professionals who run an award-winning resource* **blog**. *Here they provide free materials, advice, lesson plans, pedagogical conversation, website reviews, and more to all who drop by. The free newsletters and website articles help thousands of teachers, homeschoolers, and those serious about finding the best way to maneuver the minefields of technology in education.*

*Throughout this text, we refer to Common Core State Standards. We refer to a license granted for *"...a limited, non-exclusive, royalty-free license to copy, publish, distribute, and display the Common Core State Standards for purposes that support the Common Core State Standards Initiative. These uses may involve the Common Core State Standards as a whole or selected excerpts or portions.*

Table of Contents

Introduction

Technology Scope and Sequence

Lesson Plans

Appendices

Articles

Posters

Lesson #1—Introduction

Vocabulary	Problem solving	Big Idea
Double-click *Headphones* *Internet start page* *Keyboard* *Monitor* *Mouse button* *Mouse wheel* *Space bar* *Tower* *Website*	*What if double-click doesn't work (push enter)* *What if monitor doesn't work (turn power on)* *What if computer doesn't work?* *What if sound doesn't work?* *What if mouse doesn't work?* *I got off website (use back arrow)*	***Help students develop an awareness of computer components, fundamental hardware issues, and basic computer operations***
Time Required *45 minutes*	**NETS-S Standards** *5a; 6a*	**CC Standards** *Anchor Standards*

Essential Question
How do I use the computer?

Overview

Materials

    Internet, class rules, mouse websites

Teacher Preparation

- Talk with classroom teacher so you tie into their conversations
- Have a list of class rules that have worked in past years. Have a marker to add student suggestions to list
- Have mouse websites on class internet start page
- Test equipment so to be sure everything works
- Have several parent helpers (if possible) on early tech lessons
- Is class shorter than 45 minutes? Highlight items most important to your integration with core classroom studies and leave the rest for 'later'

Steps

    _____Tour classroom so students are comfortable with the place they'll visit every week. Share bulletin boards, printer, picture gallery, and more. Take your time.

    _____Explain rules—have them on wall. Let students ask questions and add rules they think will help class go better for everyone. Hand write them onto your posted list. Make sure this list includes group discussion rules such as 1) listen to others speak, 2) take turns speaking, 3) wait to be called on before beginning.

    _____Gather students on carpet and discuss why students use technology. Take student ideas. Do they have computers? What do they use them for?

    _____Have students move to their stations. Notice station number. Notice each computer is separate from others. Notice headphones, CPU, keyboard, mouse, monitor.

    _____Explain that they always keep hands to themselves and respect the work of others.

_____Explain good posture—body straight, hands on keyboard, elbows at side, keyboard in front, mouse to side.

_____Review how to hold mouse—finger on each button, palm at bottom, thumb on side.

_____Practice mouse skills—left/right button, double click, wheel.

_____Open internet on SmartScreen and explain what the 'internet' is, how to use it, not to use without permission. Explain what class internet start page is (see article at the end of this Lesson). Show students where websites are found.

_____Have mouse websites (see appendix) on class internet start page (see mine as sample at http://www.protopage.com/askatechteacher#Untitled/Kindergarten). Demo first so students see how to use websites, then let them explore.

_____As you teach, incorporate lesson vocabulary. Check this line if you did that today!

Assessment Strategies
- *Anecdotal*

_____Continually throughout class, check for understanding. Expect students to solve problems and make decisions.

_____Remind students to transfer knowledge to classroom or home.

_____Tuck chairs under desk, headphones over tower; leave station as you found it.

Trouble-shooting:
- *Should you switch mouse buttons for left-handed students? Read article at end of lesson.*
- *Parents confused over children and computers? Review article at end of lesson.*
- *You have print book and need website? Pick grade level and search (Alt+F) name on https://askatechteacher.wordpress.com/great-websites-for-kids/.*

Extension:
- *Read article at end of this lesson for a variety of web-based tools to assist with parent communications.*
- *If this lesson doesn't work for your student group, use one from **How to Jumpstart the Inquiry-based Classroom.** It has 5 additional projects for Kindergarten (and all grades) aligned with the SL curriculum.*

More Information:
- *Questions? Go to http://askatechteacher.com*
- *Kindergarten teaching wiki: http://smaatechk-3.wikispaces.com/This+Week+in+Tech—Kindergarten*
- *PDF: See appendix for bonus websites*
- *Follow keyboard lessons in K-8 Keyboard Curriculum (http://ow.ly/j6GH8*
- *Full digital citizenship curriculum for kindergarten available here (http://www.structuredlearning.net/book/k-8-digital-citizenship-curriculum/)*

If you don't get through everything, check completed items so you know what to get back to when you have time on later lessons. I find as I focus on the central idea of a lesson, clarifying questions sometimes take more time than I'd expect. I'm fine with that. There'll be lessons later that move faster than I planned.

MOUSE CONTROL

Single Click:
Select

Double Click:
Open

Right Click:
Drop-down menu

Using an Internet Start Page

An internet start page is the first page that comes up when students select the internet icon. It should include everything students visit on a daily basis (typing websites, research locations, sponge sites) as well as information specific to the current project, class guidelines, the day's 'to do' list, and a  calculator. It is one of the great ways teachers can make internetting simpler and safer for their students.

Mine includes oft-used websites, blog sites, a To Do list, search tools, email, a calendar of events, pictures of interest, rss feeds of interest, weather, news, a graffiti wall and more. Yours will be different. I used protopage.com, but you can use netvibes or Symbaloo.

 Start pages are an outreach of the ever-more-popular social networking. They typically have a huge library of custom fields to individualize any home page. And, they're all simple. Don't be intimidated.

When you get yours set up, on the To Do list, put what the child should do to start each computer time. This gives them a sense of independence, adultness, as they get started while you're wrapping something else up.

Should Lefties Use Right Hands for Mousing Around

Dear Otto is a column in my blog (http://askatechteacher.com) where I answer questions I get from readers about teaching tech. For privacy, I use only first names.

Here's a great question I got from Evelyn:

> *I am a Computer Teacher for Early Education (3 & 4 year old) and also Elementary students. My question to you is if a child is left handed, should you teach them to use their mouse with their left hand?*

A: I've seen lots of different answers, but there's only one that makes sense to me: Allow students to use the hand they're most comfortable with. If they want to use the left, I set the mouse up so it works for them. Often, it's a shared station, so I help the student get used to reversing the mouse buttons themselves. If that's enough to convince them to use the right hand, so be it, but sometimes, they are happy to take the time to visit the control panel and set the mouse up to suit their needs.

By allowing students to choose, I first don't let my prejudices influence how they learn. I don't want them to go one way because I told them to. I want them to make up their minds and act in their own best interests. This also prevents me from interfering with the parenting they receive at home. Moms and dads may have strong opinions on this subject and nudge their children accordingly. I don't want to interfere with that when experience tells me it doesn't make any difference.

What do you do with your lefties?

What Parents Should Know About Computers and the Internet

After fifteen years teaching tech in a classroom and online, I can tell you without a doubt that educating your child can be done more efficiently and with better results by **using technology to extend their scholastic reach**. Why?

- *Research is more productive. Students find information they want from home or the library on the topic being covered.*
- *Communication is easier using collaborative tools like wikis, Google Tools. Multiple students can work on a project at once, then embed the result into a digital portfolio.*
- *Web tools like Twitter can teach writing skills in ways kids will hear.*

So how do you make sure your child's internet experience is positive? Here are a few simple rules to help you maneuver that minefield:

- Youngsters should go on the internet only around you until they're mature enough to understand the concept of pulsing, sparkly ads. That's fifth grade, maybe Middle School. When they get distracted, be there to rein them in. Explain what happened and how to not let it repeat in the future. Show them the *Back* button that will return them to the screen they came from. Show them what ads look like on their favorite pages so they know what to avoid.
- Have a collection of ad-free child-friendly websites like Starfall for reading, and Zoopz and Game Goo for logical thinking. I try to offer only ad-free sites in the classroom, but they're hard to find. These three are exceptional.
- Filter internet sites. I never recommend unlimited internet access for any age.
- If your child has been online without you (because you considered them mature enough), don't be afraid to check history to see where they went. You're not spying; you're making sure everything is OK.
- Don't worry that your child will physically break the computer or delete an important program. It's harder than you think to mess up a computer. I have twenty-six in my lab and it's rare that students have forced me to reformat a drive (what you must do if the computer gets really messed up).
- As you see which sites your child likes to visit, put them on Favorites or an internet start page. At some point, you can allow them to access any websites on either. They'll appreciate knowing these websites are safe. Do continue to supervise. They still could have pop-ups or links to dangerous locations.

How to Use Web-based Tools to Communicate with Parents

I've been teaching for over twenty years in different schools, different communities, but one factor transcends grades, classes, and culture: Parents want to be involved with their child's school. Parent-teacher communication is vital and in my experience, the number one predictor of success for a student. But parents can't always get to the classroom to see what's written on the bulletin boards. It's not lack of interest. More likely, they're doing that 8-5 thing that insures the future of their families.

Knowing the importance of parent involvement, I feel my job as a teacher includes not just lessons I share with students, but keeping my parents informed on classroom happenings. I need to be as transparent as possible, get information out to parents in a manner they understand and a format they can access. If I could tape my classes and post them on YouTube or offer a live class feed, I would. But I can't, so I try other creative ideas.

Class website

This is gives me a chance to communicate class activities, pictures, homework, and extra credit opportunities--all the details that go into class--with parents. This is a parent's first stop to understanding what's going on in class.

Class wiki

This is student-directed, student-centered. Students post summaries of their tech class, examples of work, projects they've completed. Parents see the class through the students' eyes, as do I, which assures me that what I think happened, did.

Twitter

I love tweets because they're quick, 140 character summaries of activities, announcements, events. They take no time to read and are current.

Emails

I send lots of these out with reminders, updates, FAQs, discussions of issues that could be confusing to parents. I often ask if I'm sending too many, but my parents insist they love them.

Open door

I'm available every day after school, without an appointment. Because I have so many other ways to stay in touch, my classroom rarely gets so crowded that I can't deal with everyone who stops by.

Lesson #2—Hardware

Vocabulary	Problem solving	Big Idea
Backspace Digital Enter Escape Keyboard Monitor Mouse buttons Spacebar Tower power Transfer	*My mouse doesn't work (move it around to wake it up)* *Double-click doesn't work (push enter)* *Mouse button doesn't work (push left one, not the right)* *My volume doesn't work (plugged in? Check volume control? Do you have the right headphones on?)* *Computer doesn't work (power on?)*	***Understand and use technology systems***
Time Required *45 minutes*	**NETS-S Standards** *4a, 6c*	**CCSS** *Anchor standards*

Essential Question
How can I use technology without getting stuck?

Overview

Materials

Internet, mouse websites, sample computer parts

Teacher Preparation

- Talk with classroom teacher so you can tie into their inquiry
- Have computer hardware problems set up at several stations if you're doing extension
- Have a computer opened up if you're doing extension
- Have several parent helpers (if possible) on early tech lessons
- Is class shorter than 45 minutes? Highlight items most important to integration with core classroom studies and leave rest for 'later'.

Steps

_____Review keyboard—most common keys. There are fifteen you'll want to cover throughout the year (see diagram at end of lesson).

_____Review parts of computer (see next pages). Have students touch and feel them at their station. Follow cords to connections for CPU, mouse, keyboard, monitor. Point out power buttons. Put on headphones. Notice how you can tell parts work (i.e., mouse light is on if your system has that, headphones are plugged in, Tower Power is lit).

_____Relate hardware to problems they might have, i.e., audio doesn't work because headphones aren't plugged in. Remind students they are problem-solvers. Before asking for help, try to solve themselves.

_____Revisit mouse websites. Remind students correct way to use internet.

Assessment Strategies
- *Anecdotal observation*
- *Followed directions*
- *Displayed critical thinking*
- *Understood tech hardware*

_____As you teach, incorporate lesson vocabulary. Check this line if you did that today!

_____Continually throughout class, check for understanding.

_____Remind students to transfer knowledge to classroom or home.

_____Tuck chairs under desk, headphones over tower; leave station as you found it.

Trouble-shooting:

- *If there are lots of hardware issues, handle a few this week and more in later weeks.*
- *You have print book and need website? Pick grade level and search (Alt+F) name on https://askatechteacher.wordpress.com/great-websites-for-kids/.*

Extension:

- *Set several stations up with hardware problems; see if students can solve them.*
- *Have a computer open and show students insides.*
- *Replace this lesson with Kindergarten lesson #4 in curriculum extendors: Mouse Practice (http://www.structuredlearning.net/book/k-6-curriculum-extender/).*

More Information:

- *Lesson questions? Go to http://askatechteacher.com*
- *Kindergarten teaching wiki: http://smaatechk-3.wikispaces.com/This+Week+in+Tech—Kindergarten*
- *PDF: See appendix for bonus websites*
- *Follow keyboard lessons in K-8 Keyboard Curriculum (http://ow.ly/j6GH8)*

If you don't get through everything, check completed items so you know what to get back to when you have time on later lessons. I find as I focus on the central idea of a lesson, clarifying questions sometimes take more time than I'd expect. I'm fine with that. There'll be lessons later that move faster than I planned.

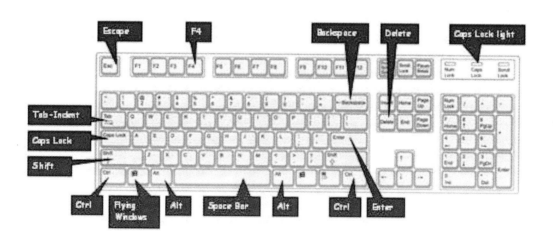

IMPORTANT KEYBOARD KEYS

Parts of the Computer

Name each part of the computer hardware system on the line next to it and label it as an 'input' device or an 'output' device.

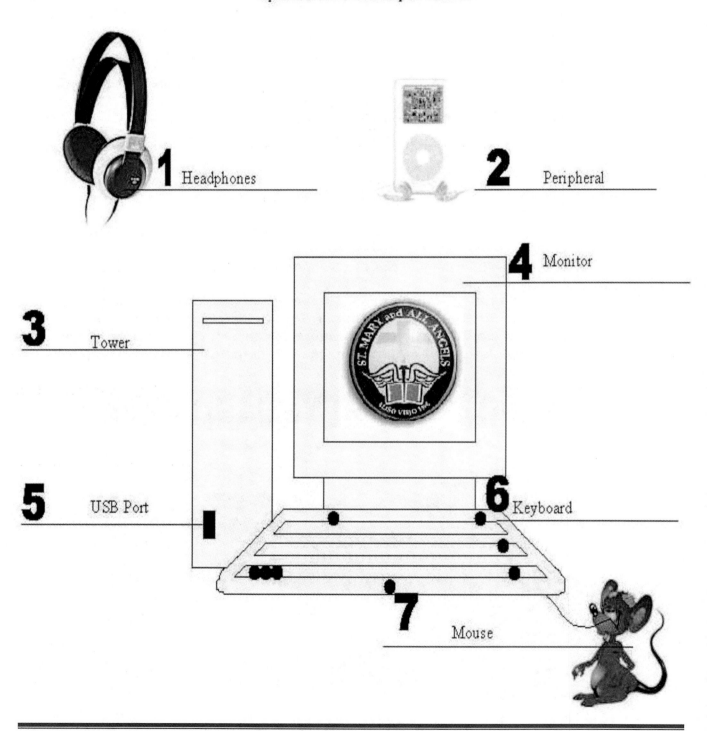

1 Headphones

2 Peripheral

4 Monitor

3 Tower

5 USB Port

6 Keyboard

7 Mouse

Lesson #3—Tools and Toolbars

Vocabulary	Problem solving	Big Idea
Click Desktop Drag Icon Keyboard Mouse Symbol Tool Tool bar	Monitor doesn't work (check power) Headphones don't work (plugged in?) Volume doesn't' work Computer doesn't work Double-click doesn't work (push enter) How do I close a program (File-exit) Can't find a tool (is it nested under others? Or at the bottom of screen?)	Select and use applications effectively and productively
Time Required 45 minutes	**NETS-S Standards** 4b, 6a	**CCSS** Anchor standards

Essential Question
How do tools and toolbars organize technology?

Overview
Materials

Internet, drawing program, mouse websites, letter websites

Teacher Preparation
- Know which letters students are covering in classroom
- Have required websites on class start page
- Test equipment—know what doesn't work
- Have parent helpers (if possible) on all early tech lessons
- Is class shorter than 45 minutes? Highlight items most important to your integration with core classroom studies and leave the rest for 'later'.

Steps

_____Explain proper care and feeding of computer:

- *No food or drink around computer*
- *No banging on keyboard*
- *Never touch neighbor's station (keyboard, monitor, mouse, etc.)*

_____Review hardware problems.

_____Open drawing program like KidPix (or Pixie, Paint, Kerpoof, free TuxPaint) with teacher assistance as needed. Show students where icon is located on desktop or start button.

_____Discuss tools and toolbars—they are symbols used to make technology easier.

_____Find pencil on tool bar; select pencil, crayon, chalk or marker at bottom and click.

_____Practice with tools; use five colors. Draw letters being discussed in class.

_____Discuss which mouse skills are used, i.e., 'drag' to use pencil.

_____As you teach, incorporate lesson vocabulary. Check this line if you did that today!

_____Continually throughout class, check for understanding. Expect students to solve problems and make decisions.

_____Remind students to transfer knowledge to classroom or home.

_____Close down to desktop. Tuck chairs under desk, headphones over tower; leave station as you found it.

Assessment Strategies
- *Observation*
- *Used tools and toolbars*
- *Joined class discussions*

Trouble-shooting:
- *Occasionally when students have difficulty doing what you are teaching, ask why. And listen. You may be surprised by the answer.*
- *When students have a techie problem, guide them to solving it without doing for them. They want to be independent—help them do that.*
- *You have print book and need website? Pick grade level and search (Alt+F) name on https://askatechteacher.wordpress.com/great-websites-for-kids/.*
- *Sometimes you need more than one week for a lesson. No worries. There are 32 lessons in text, 35ish in school year. Feel free to stretch a lesson a week or more.*

Extension:
- *Go to 'letter' websites like Starfall Letters, Bembo's Zoo, Find the letter (Google name for website address) to support class discussions.*
- *If this lesson doesn't work for your student group, use one from **How to Jumpstart the Inquiry-based Classroom.** It has 5 additional projects for Kindergarten (and all grades) aligned with the SL curriculum.*

More Information:
- *Lesson questions? Go to http://askatechteacher.com*
- *Kindergarten co-teaching wiki: http://smaatechk-3.wikispaces.com/This+Week+in+Tech—Kindergarten*
- *PDF: See appendix for bonus websites*
- *Follow keyboard lessons in K-8 Keyboard Curriculum (http://ow.ly/j6GH8)*
- *Full digital citizenship curriculum for kindergarten available here (http://www.structuredlearning.net/book/k-8-digital-citizenship-curriculum/)*

If you don't get through everything, check completed items so you know what to get back to when you have time on later lessons. I find as I focus on the central idea of a lesson, clarifying questions sometimes take more time than I'd expect. I'm fine with that. There'll be lessons later that move faster than I planned.

Do You Make These 9 Mistakes

...with your students/child's computer education?

1. Show how to do something rather than allowing her/him to discover
2. Do for them rather than let them do it
3. Say 'no' too often (or the other enthusiasm-killer, Don't touch!)
4. Don't take them seriously
5. Take technology too seriously. It's a tool, meant to make life easier. Nothing more.
6. Underestimate their abilities
7. Over-estimate their abilities
8. Give up too quickly
9. Think there's only one way to do stuff on the computer

I promise—none of these are necessary to thrive in technology. Children walk in the classroom loving learning. They can't break most computer parts. They *want* to try things out and do it themselves.

Let them. They may discover a Better Mousetrap.

After fifteen years, I still learn from my students. Children are serious about having fun. It's one of their jobs. Technology is how they do this. Feel free to join them. You'll be surprised how much they know.

But, sometimes, they need help. Offer it with a guiding hand.

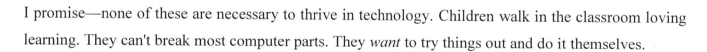

Lesson #4—Introduction to Keyboarding

Vocabulary	Problem solving	Big Idea
back space	Volume doesn't work (use control on headphones or systray)	*I want to type faster than I think*
browser	Double-click doesn't work (push enter)	
caps lock	How do I exit a program (file-exit)	
double click	I don't know where the keys are (that's why you're practicing)	
icons		
internet		
log on	I lost my website (use back button or tab on browser)	
palette		
posture	I won a computer! (Really?)	
tool bar	Can't find program (check desktop)	
tools		

Time Required	NETS-S Standards	CCSS
45 minutes	*2a, 4b*	*CCSS.ELA-Literacy.W.K.1*

Essential Question

How can I learn to type fast enough it doesn't slow down my thinking?

Overview

Materials

Internet, keyboard program, drawing program (i.e., KidPix)

Teacher Preparation

- Links for Brown Bear, TuxPaint, KidPix, Kerpoof on class internet start page
- Talk with classroom teacher so you can tie drawing into inquiry
- Have several parent helpers (if possible) on early tech lessons
- Is class shorter than 45 minutes? Highlight items most important to classroom studies and leave the rest for 'later'.

Steps

_____Introduce keyboard skills via Big Brown Bear Typing (Google for address). This focuses on key placement—nothing else. That's a great way to start kindergartners.

_____Discuss keyboarding with students. Have they seen parents use a keyboard—or siblings? What for? Why are keys not in alphabetic order? How have students used the keyboard at home or in preschool? Discuss how the keyboard is used in school—to share information with others, write student opinion about topics, share their preference (i.e., *My favorite animal is...*).

_____Before beginning, review hints on next pages about proper keyboard habits. A note: These should be doled out throughout the year when students are ready for them.

_____Before starting, review proper internet skills:

- *Sites are found on class internet start page. Review how to get there*
- *Only go to site that's linked*

- *Don't go to glitzy ads or other websites*
- *Use tab on browser to get back to class start page*
- *Notice symbols that represent the 'internet', this page, other items*

_____If computers aren't logged in, help students accomplish this.

_____Demo Big Brown Bear before students start.

_____Observe posture as they play.

_____Done? Move on to drawing program (KidPix or TuxPaint or Kerpoof—Google for addresses). Open program independently today.

_____Explore with paint tool and paint color palette; try many brushes.

_____Discuss which mouse skills are being used, i.e., drag skills, double click.

_____As you teach, incorporate lesson vocabulary. Check this line if you did that today!

_____Continually throughout class, check for understanding. Expect students to make their own decisions.

Assessment Strategies
- *Observation*
- *Followed directions*
- *Understood keyboarding*

_____Close program. Leave station as students found it—headphones over CPU, monitor on, nothing open on desktop.

_____Remind students to transfer knowledge to classroom or home.

Trouble-shooting:
- *Problem with double-click? Remind students to push enter.*
- *You have print book and need website? Pick grade level and search (Alt+F) name on* https://askatechteacher.wordpress.com/great-websites-for-kids/*.*
- *Sometimes you need more than one week for a lesson. No worries. There are 32 in the text, 35ish in the school year. Feel free to stretch a lesson a week or more.*

Extension:
- *Unplug headphones to see if students can solve this problem.*
- *This lesson is preparatory for noted Common Core standard. If time, have students write a couple of words about a topic on their canvas.*
- *If this lesson doesn't work for your students, use one from* **How to Jumpstart the Inquiry-based Classroom.** *It has 5 more projects aligned with SL curriculum.*

More Information:
- *Lesson questions? Go to* http://askatechteacher.com
- *Kindergarten teaching wiki:* http://smaatechk-3.wikispaces.com/This+Week+in+Tech—Kindergarten
- *PDF: See appendix for bonus websites*
- *Follow keyboard lessons in* K-8 Keyboard Curriculum *(*http://ow.ly/j6GH8*)*

If you don't get through everything, check completed items so you know what to get back to when you have time on later lessons. I find as I focus on the central idea of a lesson, clarifying questions sometimes take more time than I'd expect. I'm fine with that. There'll be lessons later that move faster than I planned.

Assume the Position

Great Keyboarding Hints for K-2

1. Keep keyboard centered in front of student, mouse to right (or left for lefties). Students want to push keyboard away to concentrate on mouse. Don't let them.

2. Have student tuck elbows against their sides. This keeps hands in the right spot—home row

3. Use thumb for space bar

4. Curl fingers over home row—they're cat claws, not dog paws

5. Use inside fingers for inside keys, outside for outside keys

6. Use finger closest to key needed. Sounds simple, but this isn't what usually happens with beginners.

7. Play keyboard like a piano (or violin, or guitar, or recorder). You'd never use pointer for all keys

8. Fingers move, not hands. Anchor hands to f and j

9. Don't use caps lock for capitals! Use shift

10. Keep hands to self. Don't touch other's mouse, keyboard, monitor. This gives students a sense of responsibility over their station, knowing no one can touch it but them

Lesson #5—Tools and Toolbars II

Vocabulary	Problem solving	Big Idea
background caps lock headphones icon posture screen shot software space bar stamp symbol tool bar tools volume control web-based	*How do I open a program (double click the desktop icon)* *How do I close a program (file-exit or X in the upper right corner)* *Computer doesn't work (wake up mouse)* *Monitor doesn't work (check power)* *Shift doesn't work (is caps lock on?)* *Volume doesn't work (are headphones plugged in? Do you have the right headphones?)* *Why are there icons for some programs and not others?*	*Computer programs have similar tools and toolbars. This makes technology easier to use*
Time Required *45 minutes*	**NETS-S Standards** *4a, 6a*	**CCSS** *CCSS.ELA-Literacy.SL.K*

Essential Question
How can the program layout help me communicate my message?

Overview

Materials

Internet, keyboarding program, drawing program

Teacher Preparation
- Have drawing program link on class internet start page
- Talk with classroom teacher so you can tie drawing into class inquiry
- Have parent helpers (if possible) on early tech lessons
- Is your class shorter than 45 minutes? Highlight items most important to your integration with core classroom studies and leave the rest for 'later'.

Steps

_____Warm up with keyboard practice using installed software or an typing site (like Brown Bear). I mix these up throughout year—sometimes software, sometimes online.

_____If computers aren't logged in, help students accomplish this. Discuss why there is a user name and password.

_____Review computer parts and how to solve problems related to them:

- *CPU and power button*
- *Monitor and power button*

- *Mouse—right/left button, wheel in center*
- *Keyboard*
- *Headphones—volume control for headphones*

_____Remind students to use correct posture at computer:

- *hands on their own side of keyboard*
- *legs in front of body*
- *feet in front of body*
- *body centered in front of computer*

_____Observe and guide as they keyboard.

_____Discuss tools and toolbars—symbols. How do tools, toolbars, symbols make technology clearer and easier to use?

_____As students share their thoughts, remind them to follow agreed-upon rules for discussions (e.g., listening to others and taking turns speaking).

_____Students open drawing program (KidPix, Pixie, Paint, TuxPaint, Kerpoof) with adult assistance as required. If using web-based Kerpoof, take a few minutes to remind students of internet safety.

_____Introduce backgrounds, stamps, stickers. Have students create a drawing to support a unit being discussed in class. This is practice only. They will print next week.

_____A note: It's a good idea to spend two weeks on projects—one to introduce, the second for printing/saving. Students will feel confident and proud when they know what they're doing the second week.

_____In sample inset, students found a background that fit 'My Home Town' (theme they were discussing in class). They added stamps and stickers to support their ideas.

_____Have students add their names.

_____Discuss which mouse skills are being used, i.e., drag skills.

_____Discuss how ideas are communicated with a picture rather than words. How does that relate to discussion of symbols, tools, toolbars?

_____As you teach, incorporate lesson vocabulary. Check this line if you did that today!

_____Continually throughout class, expect students to solve problems and make decisions.

_____Close program as independently as possible. They will save-print next week.

Assessment Strategies
- *Anecdotal observation*
- *Understood symbolic nature of tools, toolbars*
- *Joined class discussions*
- *Remembered skills learned in earlier weeks*
- *Attempted to solve own problems?*
- *Completed project*

_____Remind students to transfer knowledge to the classroom or home.

_____Tuck chairs under desk, headphones over tower; leave station as you found it.

Trouble-shooting:
- *Students can't find stamps/stickers they want. Provide strategies for searching, i.e., limit the number of categories they search.*
- *Drawing program won't allow saving? Take a screen shot and save that (using Jing, Snippet, or similar).*
- *Students turn monitors off so they don't have to figure out how to close down programs? Have students leave monitors on at end of class.*
- *You have print book and need website? Pick grade level and search (Alt+F) name on https://askatechteacher.wordpress.com/great-websites-for-kids/.*

Extension:
- *Add one sentence to describe picture, using good grammar and spelling (caps lock is a nice strategy at this age).*
- *Offer websites that tie into classroom discussion for those who finish early.*
- *If this lesson doesn't work for your student group, use one from* **How to Jumpstart the Inquiry-based Classroom.** *It has 5 additional projects for Kindergarten (and all grades) aligned with the SL curriculum.*

More Information:
- *Lesson questions? Go to http://askatechteacher.com*
- *Kindergarten teaching wiki: http://smaatechk-3.wikispaces.com/This+Week+in+Tech—Kindergarten*
- *PDF: See appendix for bonus websites*
- *Follow keyboard lessons in K-8 Keyboard Curriculum (http://ow.ly/j6GH8)*

If you don't get through everything, check completed items so you know what to get back to when you have time on later lessons. I find as I focus on the central idea of a lesson, clarifying questions sometimes take more time than I'd expect. I'm fine with that. There'll be lessons later that move faster than I planned.

Computer User's Haiku
Chaos reigns within.
Reflect, repent, and reboot.
Order shall return.

Lesson #6—Tools and Toolbars III

Vocabulary	Problem solving	Big Idea
Animation Drag and drop Escape Home row Keyboarding Nested Network Posture Text tool Toolbars Tools	Double-click doesn't work? (push enter) What if computer doesn't work? How do I close a program (file-exit or X in upper right corner) How do I drag and drop (click and hold with left mouse button) I can't find tool (look on toolbars to left and bottom) Why do I need my last name in file name (so it's easier to find)	*Computer programs have similar tools and toolbars. This makes technology easier to understand and use*
Time Required *45 minutes*	**NETS-S Standards** *4c, 6b*	**CCSS** *Anchor standards*

Essential Question
How do tools and toolbars organize technology?

Overview

Materials

Internet, printer, keyboard program, drawing program

Teacher Preparation

- Chat with classroom teacher to find a project that ties into inquiry
- Is class shorter than 45 minutes? Highlight items most important to your integration with core classroom studies and leave the rest for 'later'

Steps

_____Practice keyboarding with installed software or online program. Watch posture, hand position, elbows at sides.

_____Review hardware. Discuss common problems generated from hardware.

_____Students will draw a picture that ties in with class inquiry. Remember toolbars and tools used last week (background, text, stamps)? Use those.

_____Open drawing program with assistance (as needed).

_____Notice tools and toolbars used last week. Do students notice any others? We will get to most of these before year end.

_____Recreate drawing from last week. Discuss tools and toolbars used (in this case, from KidPix):

- *background tool*
- *stamp tool*
- *animation tool*

- *text tool*

_____Remind students they have used these tools before. Have them work as independently as possible.

_____As you teach, incorporate lesson vocabulary. Check this line if you did that today!

_____Continually throughout class, check for understanding.

_____Save to network folder with student last name and print (with assistance).

_____Why is it important to put student name in file name? Demonstrate a search using student name. See how their files show up even if they didn't save it right—as long as it's on the network? Putting a last name in file name makes it harder to lose work.

_____Remind students to transfer knowledge to classroom or home.

_____Tuck chairs under desk, headphones over tower; leave station as you found it.

Trouble-shooting:
- *Some Tools are 'nested' beneath other tools. Explain how to find 'nested' tools.*
- *You have print book and need website? Pick grade level and search (Alt+F) name on https://askatechteacher.wordpress.com/great-websites-for-kids/.*
- *Sometimes you need more than one week for a lesson. No worries. There are 32 lessons in text, 40ish in the school year. Feel free to stretch a lesson a week or more.*

Extension:
- *Have drawing tie into class inquiry into letters. Find stamps that fit those letters.*
- *If this lesson doesn't work for your student group, use one from **How to Jumpstart the Inquiry-based Classroom.** It has 5 additional projects for Kindergarten (and all grades) aligned with the SL curriculum.*

More Information:
- *Lesson questions? Go to http://askatechteacher.com*
- *Kindergarten teaching wiki: http://smaatechk-3.wikispaces.com/This+Week+in+Tech—Kindergarten*
- *PDF: See appendix for bonus websites*
- *Follow keyboard lessons in K-8 Keyboard Curriculum (http://ow.ly/j6GH8)*

If you don't get through everything, check completed items so you know what to get back to when you have time on later lessons. I find as I focus on the central idea of a lesson, clarifying questions sometimes take more time than I'd expect. I'm fine with that. There'll be lessons later that move faster than I planned.

Lesson #7—Math and Pumpkins I

Vocabulary	Problem solving	Big Idea
File *Fill* *Home row* *Keyboarding* *Oops Guy* *Palette* *Sections* *Symbol* *Task bar* *Texture fills* *Tool bar*	*Double-click doesn't work? (push enter)* *Program disappears? (check taskbar)* *What is today's date? (hover mouse over clock in lower right corner)* *I can't fit my name on page (move letters—and plan ahead next time)* *Color flows out of section (attach it at edges)* *I goofed (try Oops Guy—but he goes back only one step)*	*I can use pictures to do math*
Time Required *45 minutes*	**NETS-S Standards** *1a, 4b*	**CCSS** *Measurement and data*

Essential Question
How does art help me figure out math?

Overview

Materials

Internet, keyboard program, drawing program

Teacher Preparation

- Talk with classroom teacher about math: Are students able to divide a whole? How about counting?
- Is class shorter than 45 minutes? Highlight items most important to your integration with core classroom studies and leave the rest for 'later'.

Steps

_____Use installed keyboard software or online program to practice key placement.

_____Observe student posture: hands on keyboard, elbows at sides, legs in front of body, feet not under bottom.

_____Open drawing program (i.e., KidPix, Paint, Tux Paint or Kerpoof—Google for addresses). Students will practice a Halloween project today using paint brush and fills. They print next week.

_____Demonstrate project for students. Notice shape is divided into pieces, like a pie, or a pizza (see inset). Depending upon where students are in their math studies, 1) count the pieces, and/or 2) show how all the pieces make a whole.

_____Open drawing program (we use KidPix in this example). Students should be able to do this unassisted.

_____Select desired color from palette; select a brush and draw a pumpkin (or other Halloween symbol). Add a stem and face using different brushes. Separate symbol into 3-4 sections (see inset). Let students make mistakes, try different colors, experiment with brushes. Show how 'Oops' guy works. Remind them to 'oops' immediately when they don't like what they did. Show how to 'blow up' and start over. It's OK. There's lots of time.

_____Show how fills work—three buckets and options. Have students select paint bucket tool, first bucket, one color from palette. Fill sections with different texture fills (see inset).

_____Drag and drop letters for student name. See how they must leave room for entire name. Show how to adjust if spacing is off.

_____Encourage students to think critically as they make decisions about creating this drawing.

_____Don't worry if not finished—we won't print today.

_____Continually throughout class, check for understanding. Expect students to solve problems and make decisions.

_____Remind students to transfer knowledge to classroom or home.

_____As you teach, incorporate lesson vocabulary. Check this line if you did that today!

_____Close program without assistance. Tuck chairs under desk, headphones over tower; leave station as it was.

Assessment Strategies

- *Did they remember skills learned in earlier weeks?*
- *Understood math concepts of dividing picture*
- *Understood the process used and the goal*
- *Attempted to solve their problems*

Trouble-shooting:

- *Some Tools are 'nested' beneath other tools. Explain how to find 'hidden' tools.*
- *Student can't finish? It doesn't matter. If working on tools, toolbars, mouse skills, they're succeeding!*
- *Paint bucket fill flows from one part to another? Complete dividing lines.*
- *Student can't fit their name in the space? Discuss planning and layout with students so they can fix it next week.*
- *Ask students to try to solve problems themselves before asking for assistance.*
- *You have print book and need website? Pick grade level and search (Alt+F) name on https://askatechteacher.wordpress.com/great-websites-for-kids/.*

Extension:

- *Sometime early in the school year, visit classroom and explain to students how what they do at class computer pod (or iPads, netbooks, other tech devices) is the same as what they do in lab, just smaller. See sheet at end of this lesson for visit ideas.*

- Tie this lesson into class math discussions by comparing measurable attributes of pumpkin pieces and discussing differences.
- Have websites on class internet start page that tie into classroom inquiry for students who finish early
- If this lesson doesn't work for your student group, use one from **How to Jumpstart the Inquiry-based Classroom.** It has 5 additional projects for Kindergarten (and all grades) aligned with the SL curriculum.

More Information:
- Lesson questions? Go to http://askatechteacher.com
- Kindergarten teaching wiki: http://smaatechk-3.wikispaces.com/This+Week+in+Tech—Kindergarten
- PDF: See appendix for bonus websites
- Follow keyboard lessons in K-8 Keyboard Curriculum (http://ow.ly/j6GH8)

If you don't get through everything, check completed items so you know what to get back to when you have time on later lessons. I find as I focus on the central idea of a lesson, clarifying questions sometimes take more time than I'd expect. I'm fine with that. There'll be lessons later that move faster than I planned.

> **"A printer consists of three main parts: the case, the jammed paper tray and the blinking red light"**
> **—Anonymous**

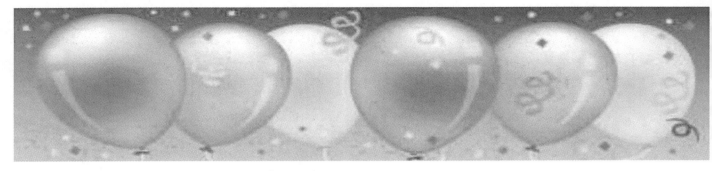

<u>Take Tech into the Classroom</u>

When classroom teacher feels students are settled into class routine enough to get started on class pod of computers, join them for center time and transfer tech class knowledge to the class.

<u>Before going:</u>

- Make sure class computers work
  - *CPU*
  - *headphones*
- Make sure computers have all required links. What are the teacher's favorites?
  - *The school website*
  - *Tech lab class internet start page*
  - *Typing practice program*
  - *Starfall*
  - *A math program*
- Make sure they are set up the same as in tech lab (or know the differences so you can explain)

<u>During visit, go over these with students:</u>

- Same rules that apply in tech class apply in classroom (add your rules):
  - *No food or drink by computers*
  - *No fooling around*
  - *No grabbing neighbor's equipment*
  - *Internet only to approved sites*
  - *Try to solve problems before asking for help (especially important because you as tech teacher won't be there to help)*
  - *Look around screen before asking for help*
  - *Leave station the way you found it*
  - *Print only with permission*
- Practice good habits every time you sit at computer
- Take questions

Lesson #8— Math and Pumpkins II

Vocabulary	Problem solving	Big Idea
Alphabet Drag and drop Escape Fill Home row Icon Log-on Nested Oops guy Screen shot Symbol Task bar Tool bar	What if double-click doesn't work(push enter key) Program gone (check taskbar) Type to Learn Jr won't type (Do you have the caps lock on?) What if paint bucket fill goes into other section (close down section) What if Animation—alphabet (dog alphabet) doesn't show (change menu with drop-down box) I goofed (Oops it right away) What's the difference between save and export?	*I can use pictures to do math*

Time Required	NETS-S Standards	CCSS
45 minutes	1a, 4b	Measurement and data

Essential Question
How does art help me figure out math?

Overview

Materials

Internet, keyboard program, drawing program

Teacher Preparation

- Talk with class teacher about math: Can students divide a whole? How about counting?
- Is class shorter than 45 minutes? Highlight items most important to your integration with core classroom studies and leave the rest for 'later'.

Steps

_____Open drawing program (KidPix, Tux Paint, Kerpoof or other—Google for addresses). Students will create, print, and save a Halloween project today using paint brush and fills.

_____Demonstrate project for students. Notice one shape is divided into pieces, like a pie, or a pizza. Depending upon where students are in their math studies, 1) count the pieces, and/or 2) show how all pieces make a whole.

_____Open drawing program (here, we use

KidPix). Students should be able to do this unassisted by now.

_____Remember skills learned and practiced last week. Display a completed project on SmartScreen. Have one student come up and share which tools were used in each part of project.

_____Select color from palette; select brush and draw pumpkin (or other Halloween symbol); add a stem, face using different brushes if desired. Separate into 3-4 sections (see inset). Remind students to 'oops' immediately after they don't like what they did. Or, 'blow up' and start over. It's OK. There's lots of time.

_____Encourage students to think critically as they make decisions about dividing drawings.

_____Use paint bucket fills. Select paint bucket tool, first bucket, one color from palette. Fill sections with different textures (see inset).

_____Drag and drop letters for student name. Remember how they must leave room for entire name. Remind how to adjust letters if spacing is off.

_____Print with assistance; save or export to network folder. What's the difference? Remember to include last name in file name.

_____Expect students to complete this project as independently as possible.

_____Those who finish early: Use keyboard program to practice key placement.

_____Observe student posture: Both hands on keyboard, elbows at sides, legs in front of body.

_____Continually throughout class, check for understanding.

_____Remind students to transfer knowledge to the classroom or home.

_____As you teach, incorporate lesson vocabulary. Check this line if you did that today!

_____Close program without assistance. Tuck chairs under desk, headphones over tower; leave station as you found it.

> ## Assessment Strategies
> - *Observation of student*
> - *Saved to digital portfolio*
> - *Completed project*
> - *Used previously-learned skills*
> - *Understood process*

Trouble-shooting:
- *Some tools are 'nested' beneath other tools. Explain how to find.*
- *Occasionally when students have difficulty doing what you are teaching, ask why. And listen. You may be surprised by the answer.*
- *Paint bucket fill flows from one part to another? Are dividing lines complete?*
- *Drawing program won't allow saving? Save a screen shot (with Jing, Snippet, similar).*
- *You have print book and need website? Pick grade level and search (Alt+F) name on https://askatechteacher.wordpress.com/great-websites-for-kids/.*

Extension:
- *Compare measurable attributes of pumpkin pieces. Discuss differences.*
- *Use this second week on Math and Pumpkins as a formative assessment. What do students remember of last week's skills?*

- *Have websites on class internet start page that tie into classroom inquiry for students who finish early*
- *Anytime you can inject tech into the class, do it! Students love seeing gadgets in action. For example—take a video of students working at their computers and upload to class website/blog/wiki.*
- *If this lesson doesn't work for your student group, use one from **How to Jumpstart the Inquiry-based Classroom.** It has 5 additional projects for Kindergarten (and all grades) aligned with the SL curriculum.*

More Information:
- *Lesson questions? Go to http://askatechteacher.com*
- *Kindergarten teaching wiki:*
  http://smaatechk-3.wikispaces.com/This+Week+in+Tech—Kindergarten
- *PDF: See appendix for bonus websites*
- *Follow keyboard lessons in K-8 Keyboard Curriculum (http://ow.ly/j6GH8)*

If you don't get through everything, check completed items so you know what to get back to when you have time on later lessons. I find as I focus on the central idea of a lesson, clarifying questions sometimes take more time than I'd expect. I'm fine with that. There'll be lessons later that move faster than I planned.

"Tell me and I forget, show me and I remember, involve me and I understand."
—Chinese Proverb

Is Keyboarding Dead?

I was on one of my tech forums—where I keep up to date on changes in education and technology—and stumbled into a heated discussion about what grade level is best to begin the focus on typing (is fifth grade too old—or too young?). Several teachers shared that keyboarding was the cornerstone of their elementary-age technology program. Others confessed their Admin wanted it eliminated as unnecessary. Still others dismissed the discussion as moot: Tools like Dragon Speak (the standard in speech recognition software) and iPhone's wildly-popular Siri mean keyboarding will soon be as useful as cursive and floppy discs.

My knee jerk reaction was *That's years off,* but it got me thinking. Is it really? Or are the fires of change about to sweep through our schools? Already, families are succumbing to the overwhelming popularity of touch screens in the guise of iPads. No typing required—just a finger poke, a sweep, and the command is executed. Those clumsy, losable styluses of your parent's era are so last generation. The day kids discover how easy it is to *tell* tech tools what they need—stick a fork in it; keyboarding will be done.

Truthfully, as someone who carefully watches ed tech trends, a discussion about the importance of keyboarding says as much about national education expectations as typing. Schools are moving away from reports and essays as methods of assessing understanding. Teachers want plays that act out a topic, student-created videos that demonstrate authentic understanding, multi-media magazines that convey a deeper message. Web-based communication tools like Voki, Animoto, and Glogster—all of which have limited typing—are *de rigeur* in every academic program that purports to be tech-savvy. Students are encouraged to use audio, visual, taped vignettes, recorded snippets—everything that ISN'T the traditional MS Word document with a bullet list of comprehensive points to convey the message. For much of what students want out of life—to call a friend, find their location on GPS, arrange a get-together, create a reminder—writing is passé. To your middle school and high school children, email is as anachronistic as snail mail is to twenty-somethings. Even texting is being shunted aside by vlogs and Skype, and note-taking—with the popularity of apps like Evernote—is now best accomplished with swipes and clicks.

That's what's killing keyboarding.

But not yet.

Certainly, voice commands can activate a software program or bring up the teacher's website to view homework, but how do you quietly talk to a computer during a lecture? Are programs like Dragon Speak and Siri capable of blocking out extraneous sounds and focusing in on the singular human voice? And don't discount the aesthetics of typing. Take me for example. I'm a K-8 technology teacher. I'm in the know about the latest and greatest in technology trends. I'm expected to try them—and use them. I write for a hobby, but I have arthritis. My doctor wants me to stop typing, switch to Dragon Speak. My modern kids are all for it, but Dragon Speak's quirkiness (like mis-typing oh-so-many words) is distracting. Plus, there's a connection between my brain and fingers that helps me think. Maybe it's as simple as I muse at the speed I type. Maybe the clackity-clack of the keys is soothing to my rattled brain. Nothing in my pedagogic research has convinced me it isn't also true for kids. If we eliminate the peaceful predictability of tapping fingers on little squares, will getting words on paper be more difficult?

I wonder.

I decided to poll my parents. Overwhelmingly, they support age-appropriate keyboard training for children as young as kindergarten. They understand that typing may be antiquated someday, but not today, or tomorrow. Until it is, they want their kids to learn it.

What do you think?

Photo credit: Beeki (http://pixabay.com/en/cress-spice-plant-keyboard-15086/)

Lesson #9—Holiday Cards With Shapes I

Vocabulary	Problem solving	Big Idea
ABC tool Alphabet Backspace Drag-and-drop Enter Escape Palette Problem-solving Spacebar Stamps Stickers	My program disappeared (check taskbar) My monitor doesn't work (check power and CPU connection) I spelled it wrong! (backspace) Foot faces wrong direction (show how to correct) I can't get my name on page (try again next week)	*Shapes are everywhere in the environment and help me understand objects.*
Time Required *45 minutes*	**NETS-S Standards** *1c, 4a*	**CCSS** *CCSS.Math.Content.K.G.A*

Essential Question
How do shapes relate to the real world?

Overview

Materials

Internet, drawing program, keyboarding program

Teacher Preparation

- What shapes are being discussed in class?
- What letters are being covered in class?
- What shapes are around your classroom?
- If you're doing Extension, 1) know what shapes are around the school, 2) have extra parent helpers.
- Is class shorter than 45 minutes? Highlight items most important to your integration with core classroom studies and leave the rest for 'later'.

Steps

_____Discuss shapes. What do students know from classroom conversations? If necessary, remind students of rules class has agreed upon for discussions—such as listening to others and taking turns speaking.

_____Point to something in classroom (i.e., a poster). What shape would it take to create that? How about a CD? What shape is that? What about the hole in the center?

_____Ask students to open their drawing program—

KidPix or TuxPaint or Kerpoof or other. Today they'll draw a Thanksgiving turkey.

_____Show a sample on screen. What shapes are required to draw a turkey?

_____Ask students which toolbar tools they'll use. Demonstrate the ones they select until they are satisfied. Model:

- *Drawing the shape (using dragging skills)*
- *Adding a face (drag-and-drop skills)*
- *Adding a short greeting (ABC tool)*
- *Adding their name (dog alphabet)*

_____Ask students to begin by finding pencil tool and circle tool. Demonstrate.

_____Select 5 colors from palette. This is hard on kindergarten fine motor skills so remind them they can practice, redo and start again next week.

_____Use stamp tool to add turkey face. In KidPix, show students how to reverse feet and ears with 'blue arrow' on tool bar, You'll be surprised how little trouble students have with this!

_____Add student name with dog alphabet.

_____Add a greeting with ABC text tool.

_____Continually throughout class, check for understanding. Expect students to make decisions.

_____Practice today; print next week. Remind students they know these skills so you expect them to try first before asking for assistance.

_____No saving today; file-exit.

_____Remind students to transfer knowledge to classroom or home.

_____As you teach, incorporate lesson vocabulary. Check this line if you did that today!

_____Those who finish: practice keyboard skills with installed software or online program like Brown Bear. Pay attention to hand position—on home row; keep elbows at sides.

_____Tuck chairs under desk, headphones over tower; leave station as you found it.

Trouble-shooting:

- *Students have trouble drawing the feathers? That's OK. It's hard on kindergarten fine motor skills. Whatever they accomplish is fine.*
- *Shapes are not filled in? Show students KidPix shape tool that's filled in.*
- *Some tools are 'nested' beneath other tools. Explain how to find.*
- *Fill flows from one part to another? Show how to connect parts.*

- You have print book and need website? Pick grade level and search (Alt+F) name on *https://askatechteacher.wordpress.com/great-websites-for-kids/*.

Extension:

- *Bring up a turkey pictures on SmartScreen. Ask students to describe where a part (i.e., the turkey mouth) is in relation to the other parts (i.e., student name) using words like **above, below, beside, in front of, behind, and next to**.*
- *Have students draw their picture with another object placed above, below, beside, in front of, behind, or next to. As you watch them draw, ask about that relationship.*
- *Send students to letter websites that tie into class discussion of letters. Here are some examples:*

  - *Find the letter*
  - *Bembo's Zoo*
  - *Starfall Letters*
  - *Find letter—3 difficulty levels*
  - *Click the Square*

- *If this lesson doesn't work for your student group, use one from **How to Jumpstart the Inquiry-based Classroom.** It has 5 additional projects for Kindergarten (and all grades) aligned with the SL curriculum.*

More Information:

- *Lesson questions? Go to http://askatechteacher.com*
- *Kindergarten teaching wiki: http://smaatechk-3.wikispaces.com/This+Week+in+Tech—Kindergarten*
- *PDF: See appendix for bonus websites*
- *Follow keyboard lessons in K-8 Keyboard Curriculum (http://ow.ly/j6GH8)*

If you don't get through everything, check completed items so you know what to get back to when you have time on later lessons. I find as I focus on the central idea of a lesson, clarifying questions sometimes take more time than I'd expect. I'm fine with that. There'll be lessons later that move faster than I planned.

"A computer does what you tell it to do, not what you want it to do."

The Secret to Teaching Tech: Delegate

There's a secret to teaching kids how to use the computer. It's called 'delegate'. I don't mean sluff off teaching to aides or parents. I'm referring to empowering students to be problem-solvers, then expect it. Here's how:

- Computers are only hard to learn if kids are *told* they are. Don't. Compare keyboarding to piano—a skill lots of kids feel good about—or one that relates to your particular group. Remove fear.

- Teach students how to do the twenty most common problems faced on a computer (more on that as they get older). Expect them to know these—do pop quizzes if that's your teaching style). Post them on the walls. Do a Problem-solving Board. Remind them if they know these, they'll have 70% less problems (that's true, too) than kids who don't know how to solve these. If they raise their hand and ask for help, play Socrates and force them to think through the answer. Sometimes I point to the wall. Sometimes I ask the class for help. Pick a way that works for you. The only solution you *can't* employ is to do it for them

- Teach students keyboard shortcuts. Does that sound like an odd suggestion? It isn't. Students learn in different ways. Some are best with menus, ribbons and mouse clicks. Some like the ease and speed of the keyboard. Give them that choice. If they know both ways, they'll pick the one that works best for them. Once they know these, they'll be twice as likely to remember how to exit a program (Alt+F4) or print (Ctrl+P).

- Let neighbors help neighbors. I resisted this for several years, thinking they'd end up chatting about non-tech topics. They don't when sufficiently motivated and interested. They are excited to show off their knowledge by helping classmates.

Lesson #10—Holiday Cards With Shapes II

Vocabulary	Problem solving	Big Idea
Export Fill Icon Log on Problem solving Square spacebar Symbol Tool Tool bar	Double-click doesn't work (push enter) Can't log on (what's user name) I can hear a program but can't see it (check another tab on browser) What's today's date? (hover mouse over clock in lower right corner) My turkey foot faces the wrong way (show students how to fix) What's the difference between save and export?	*Shapes are everywhere in the environment and help me understand objects.*
Time Required 45 minutes	**NETS-S Standards** 1c, 4a	**CCSS** CCSS.Math.Content.K.G.A

Essential Question
How do shapes relate to the real world?

Overview

Materials
Internet, drawing program, keyboard program, internet websites

Teacher Preparation
- What shapes are being discussed in class?
- What letters are being covered in class?
- What shapes are around your classroom?
- If doing Extension, know shapes around school—and have extra parent helpers
- Is class shorter than 45 minutes? Highlight items most important to your integration with core classroom studies and leave the rest for 'later'.

Steps
_____Ask students to open drawing program. Today they'll draw the turkey practiced last class, print, and export for Open House.

_____Show a sample on screen. Remind them what shapes make up a turkey.

_____Show a sample of this project on SmartScreen and have one student point out which tools they used last week. Model how to draw if needed (using dragging skills), add a face (drag-and-drop skills). Add a short greeting with text tool and their name.

_____Students know these skills so expect them to try before asking for assistance.

_____As you teach, incorporate lesson vocabulary. Check this line if you did that today!

_____Continually throughout class, check for understanding.

_____Export for Open House slideshow. Why export? What's Open House? Print.

_____Remind students to transfer knowledge to classroom or home.

_____Those who finish: Practice keyboarding with installed software or online typing program like Brown Bear. Pay attention to hand position; keep elbows at sides.

_____Done? Go to websites (which you placed on internet start page) that tie in with class discussions.

_____Tuck chairs under desk, headphones over tower; leave station as it was.

Trouble-shooting:

* *Drawing program won't allow saving? Take a screen shot and save that (using Jing, Snippet, or similar).*
* *Student can't finish? It doesn't matter to the goals we focus on with this project. If they're working on tools, toolbars, mouse skills, they're succeeding!*
* *You have print book and need website? Pick grade level and search (Alt+F) name on https://askatechteacher.wordpress.com/great-websites-for-kids/.*

Extension:

* *Bring up student turkey pictures on SmartScreen. Ask students to describe where a part (i.e., turkey) is in relation to other parts (i.e., student name) using words like above, below, beside, in front of, behind, and next to.*
* *Have students draw the turkey with another object placed above, below, beside, in front of, behind, or next to. As they draw, ask about that relationship.*
* *Instead of using the solid circle in KidPix, use empty one. Students can then use the paint bucket tool with the fill of their choice.*
* *Add a background (see sample on next pages).*
* *Use this second week as a formative assessment. What do students remember of skills practiced last week?*
* *Replace lesson with 1st Grade #4—What's a Digital Citizen—in curriculum extenders http://www.structuredlearning.net/book/k-6-curriculum-extender/ .*

More Information:

* *Lesson questions? Go to http://askatechteacher.com*
* *Kindergarten teaching wiki: http://smaatechk-3.wikispaces.com/This+Week+in+Tech—Kindergarten*
* *PDF: See appendix for bonus websites*
* *Follow keyboard lessons in K-8 Keyboard Curriculum (http://ow.ly/j6GH8)*

If you don't get through everything, check completed items so you know what to get back to when you have time on later lessons. I find as I focus on the central idea of a lesson, clarifying questions sometimes take more time than I'd expect. I'm fine with that. There'll be lessons later that move faster than I planned.

More Holiday Shapes

Lesson #11—Introduction to Google Earth

Vocabulary	Problem solving	Big Idea
Google Earth *Grid lines* *Latitude* *Longitude* *Mouse wheel* *Multimedia* *Pan* *Search engine* *Tour* *Zoom*	*Screen froze (is the program blinking on the taskbar?)* *Can't exit program (Alt+F4)* *How do I print (Ctrl+P)* *How do I save (Ctrl+S)* *Can't zoom in (click on the screen and try again)* *What time is it? (clock in monitor corner)*	***With technology, I can explore the world.***
Time Required *45 minutes*	**NETS-S Standards** *3a, 3d*	**CCSS** *CCSS.ELA-Literacy.RI.K.10*

Essential Question
How do I use technology to explore the planet?

Overview

Materials

Internet, Google Earth, keyboard program

Teacher Preparation

- Make sure Google Earth works on all computers and tours are installed
- Talk with classroom teacher about creating class tour
- Is class shorter than 45 minutes? Highlight items most important to your integration with core classroom studies and leave the rest for 'later'.

Steps

_____Warm up for 10-15 minutes with keyboarding using installed software or an online program (see appendix). I like Brown Bear.

_____Before opening Google Earth, discuss the planet—continents, oceans, other topics being discussed in class.

_____Now open Google Earth on SmartScreen. Show students where places they have discussed in class are located. Ask students where else they have explored on the planet?

_____Open grid lines in Google Earth. Show how the planet is organized so the tiniest location can be identified by a latitude and longitude. Relate this to the student's home address.

_____On SmartScreen, plug in a student address and zoom to it. Use Street View guy to stand in front of student house. Does this look familiar?

Assessment Strategies
- *Anecdotal*
- *Followed directions*
- *Displayed a sense of inquiry*
- *Understood how visual representation of globe guides understanding*

_____Explore Google Earth with the class. Show how to drag globe around, pan in and out with mouse wheel. Explain they will learn more in first grade. After you've demonstrated, let students explore.

_____After sufficient time, show one tour on SmartScreen. Use the built-in tour or one created by fifth graders (see 5th grade curriculum). Discuss as a group. Prompt for student ideas on the purpose of a Google Earth tour and what they might understand better in this manner than, say, a book.

_____Let students do it on their computers.

_____As you teach, incorporate lesson vocabulary. Check this line if you did that today!

_____Continually check for understanding.

_____Remind students to transfer knowledge to classroom or home.

_____Tuck chairs under desk, headphones over tower; leave station as you found it.

Trouble-shooting:
- *Students have difficulty using drag-and-drop to move globe? Try arrow keys.*
- *You have print book and need website? Pick grade level and search (Alt+F) name on https://askatechteacher.wordpress.com/great-websites-for-kids/.*

Extension:
- *Have students type in school or home address and watch Google Earth find it.*
- *Use Google Earth with iPad app. Let students curl into a comfortable seat and explore.*
- *Sometimes you need more than one week for a lesson. No worries. There are 32 lessons in text, 35ish in the school year. Feel free to stretch a lesson a week or more.*
- *If this lesson doesn't work for your student group, use one from **How to Jumpstart the Inquiry-based Classroom.** It has 5 additional projects aligned with SL curriculum.*

More Information:
- *Lesson questions? Go to http://askatechteacher.com*
- *Kindergarten teaching wiki: http://smaatechk-3.wikispaces.com/This+Week+in+Tech—Kindergarten*
- *PDF: See appendix for bonus websites*
- *Follow keyboard lessons in K-8 Keyboard Curriculum (http://ow.ly/j6GH8)*

If you don't get through everything, check completed items so you know what to get back to when you have time on later lessons. I find as I focus on the central idea of a lesson, clarifying questions sometimes take more time than I'd expect. I'm fine with that. There'll be lessons later that move faster than I planned.

Lesson #12—Virtual Field Trip I

Vocabulary	Problem solving	Big Idea
• Ads • Back button • Bling • Digital neighborhood • Internet start page • iPad • Link • Mouse wheel • Online • Street View Guy • Tabbed browsing • Tour • Virtual • Virtual field trip • X	• What if double-click doesn't work? (push enter) • I can't get tour to work (look around screen) • I won a million dollars on internet! • I got off of my website (click tab on browser) • I clicked an ad by accident (click back button) • I can't close the internet • I hear noise in the background (did you close last tour tab?)	*The computer is a great way to visit the world.*
Time Required *45 minutes*	**NETS-S Standards** *3a, 3d*	**CCSS** *CCSS.ELA-Literacy.RI.K.10*

Essential Question
How do I use the computer to take a Field Trip

Overview

Materials

Internet, virtual tours, iPads (if necessary)

Teacher Preparation

- Talk with teacher about an upcoming class field trip
- Have virtual tours on class internet start page
- Have websites on start page that tie into class conversations
- Is class period shorter than 45 minutes? Highlight the items most important to your integration with core classroom studies and leave the rest for 'later'.

Steps

_____Warm up for 10-15 minutes of keyboarding using installed software or an online program (see appendix). I like Big Brown Bear Typing. Remind students:

- *hands on home row*
- *legs in front of body*
- *elbows at sides*
- *feet on floor, not under bottoms*

_____Today, we take virtual tours of interesting places. <u>Here are examples</u> (<u>http://askatechteacher.wordpress.com/great-websites-for-kids/virtual-tours/</u>):

- _360 Panorama of world_
- _3D Toads and more_
- _World of Wonders_
- _Pompeii_
- _Sistine Chapel_
- _Virtual Body_
- _Virtual Farm_

- _Virtual tour of America_
- _Virtual tour (pictures) of zoo_
- _Virtual tour–undersea_
- _Virtual Zoo_
- _Walk through the Forest_
- _The White House_

_____By the way: the _White House_ isn't a link because you access it through Google Earth. Type 'White House' into 'Fly to' bar, zoom in until you melt through the roof or wall, into the building. It throws you into Street View and you start your amazing tour. Remind students of all the skills they learned last week.

_____Before starting: Remind students how to stay safe on the internet:

- _Only go to assigned websites_
- _Don't get distracted by bling_
- _Avoid ads_
- _Stay in the digital neighborhood_

_____Explore several virtual tours on the SmartScreen. Prompt for what students can see on this virtual tour that is different from pictures or teacher words? Do they feel like they've been there? Do they want to go more now that they've had this preview?

_____Let students go on several tours. Two of my favorites: Walk through the Forest and Virtual tour of America. Link tours from class internet start page for easy access (I create a Box of Links including all virtual tours).

_____Demonstrate what this means using one of the tour websites. Bring up a website and ask students, _Where is their digital neighborhood on this site? How might they wander away from the assigned website? What bling do they see that could be distracting? Where are ads? What are ads?_

_____Demonstrate how 1) to get back to assigned website with back button and tabbed browser, 2) to use back arrow if they click on the wrong website by accident, 3) to ignore ads that call for action.

_____As you teach, incorporate lesson vocabulary. Check this line if you did that today!

_____Continually throughout class, check for understanding. Expect students to solve problems and make decisions that follow class rules.

_____Close down to desktop with 'x'. Tuck chairs under desk, headphones over tower; leave station as it was.

Assessment Strategies

- _Anecdotal_
- _Related 'virtual' to reality_
- _Used previously-learned skills_
- _Used internet properly_
- _Showed good keyboarding habits_

_____Remind students to transfer knowledge to classroom or home.

Trouble-shooting:
- *You have print book and need website? Pick grade level and search (Alt+F) name on https://askatechteacher.wordpress.com/great-websites-for-kids/.*
- *Sometimes you need more than one week for a lesson. No worries. There are 32 lessons in text, 35ish in the school year. Feel free to stretch a lesson a week or more.*

Extension:
- *Do this in groups.*
- *Use iPads to explore virtual tours.*
- *Replace lesson with Kindergarten lesson #2—SmartScreen Read Aloud in curriculum extendors (http://www.structuredlearning.net/book/k-6-curriculum-extender/).*
- *Some students finish early? Provide websites on class internet start page that tie into class units of inquiry.*

More Information:
- *Lesson questions? Go to http://askatechteacher.com*
- *Kindergarten teaching wiki: http://smaatechk-3.wikispaces.com/This+Week+in+Tech—Kindergarten*
- *PDF: See appendix for bonus websites*
- *Follow keyboard lessons in K-8 Keyboard Curriculum (http://ow.ly/j6GH8)*
- *Full digital citizenship curriculum for kindergarten available here (http://www.structuredlearning.net/book/k-8-digital-citizenship-curriculum/)*

If you don't get through everything, check completed items so you know what to get back to when you have time on later lessons. I find as I focus on the central idea of a lesson, clarifying questions sometimes take more time than I'd expect. I'm fine with that. There'll be lessons later that move faster than I planned.

> **"If it's really a supercomputer, how come the bullets don't bounce off when I shoot it?"**

10 Ways to be an Inquiry-based Teacher

It's hard to run an inquiry-based classroom. Don't go into this teaching style thinking all you do is ask questions and observe answers. You have to listen with all of your senses, pause and respond to what you heard (not what you wanted to hear), keep your eye on the Big Ideas as you facilitate learning, value everyone's contribution, be aware of the energy of the class and step in when needed, step aside when required. You aren't a Teacher, rather a guide. You and the class move from question to knowledge together.

Because everyone learns differently.

Where your teacher credential classes taught you to use a textbook, now it's one of many resources. Sure, it nicely organizes knowledge week-by-week, but in an inquiry-based classroom, you may know where you're going, but not quite how you'll get there—and that's a good thing. You are no longer your mother's teacher who stood in front of rows of students and pointed to the blackboard. You operate well outside your teaching comfort zone as you try out a flipped classroom and the gamification of education and are thrilled with the results.

And then there's the issue of assessment. What students accomplish can no longer neatly be summed up by a multiple choice test. When you review what you thought would assess learning (back when you designed the unit), none measure the organic conversations the class had about deep subjects, the risk-taking they engaged in to arrive at answers, the authentic knowledge transfer that popped up independently of your class time. You realize you must open your mind to learning that occurred that you never taught—never saw coming in the weeks you stood amongst your students guiding their education.

Let me digress. I visited the Soviet Union (back when it was one nation) and dropped in on a classroom where students were inculcated with how things must be done. It was a polite, respectful, ordered experience, but without cerebral energy, replete of enthusiasm for the joy of learning, and lacking the wow factor of students independently figuring out how to do something. Seeing the end of that powerful nation, I arrived at different conclusions than the politicians and the economists. I saw a nation starved to death for creativity. Without that ethereal trait, learning didn't transfer. Without transfer, life required increasingly more scaffolding and prompting until it collapsed in on itself like a hollowed out orange.

So how do you create the inquiry-based classroom? Here's advice from a few of my efriend teachers:

1. *ask open-ended questions and be open-minded about conclusions*
2. *provide hands-on experiences*
3. *use groups to foster learning*
4. *encourage self-paced learning. Be open to the student who learns less but deeper as much as the student who learns a wider breadth*
5. *differentiate instruction. Everyone learns in their own way*
6. *look for evidence of learning in unusual places. It may be from the child with his/her hand up, but it may also be from the learner who teaches mom how to use email*
7. *understand 'assessment' comes in many shapes. It may be a summative quiz, a formative simulation, a rubric, or a game that requires knowledge to succeed. It may be anecdotal or peer-to-peer. Whatever approach shows students are transferring knowledge from your classroom to life is a legitimate assessment*
8. *be flexible. Class won't always (probably never) go as your mind's eye saw it. That's OK. Learn with students. Observe their progress and adapt to their path.*
9. *give up the idea that teaching requires control. Refer to #8—Be flexible*
10. *facilitate student learning in a way that works for them. Trust that they will come up with the questions required to reach the Big Ideas*

In the end, know that inquiry-based teaching is not about learning for the moment. You're creating life-long learners, the individuals who will solve the world's problems in ten years. Your job is to ensure they are ready.

Lesson #13—Virtual Field Trip II

Vocabulary	Problem solving	Big Idea
Arrow keys *Back button* *Bling* *Cursor* *Digital neighborhood* *Link* *Pan* *Street view guy* *Virtual* *Website* *Zoom*	*Double-click doesn't work (press enter)* *Program's gone (check task bar)* *I got off the assigned website (use back button)* *I can't find the link (where does the cursor turn into a little hand)* *Street View Guy doesn't work (are there any streets highlighted blue?)* *Street View Guy doesn't work (are there any streets highlighted blue?)*	**Technology is a great way to visit the world.**
Time Required *45 minutes*	**NETS-S Standards** *3a, 3d*	**CCSS** *CCSS.ELA-Literacy.RI.K.10*

Essential Question
How do I use technology to take a Virtual Field Trip

Overview

Materials

Internet, websites for class field trip, Google Earth, keyboard program

Teacher Preparation

- Chat with teacher to find out if there is a field trip coming up you can tie into
- Prepare several websites to visit that support the field trip
- Preview route from school to location so you know what to point out about virtual trip
- Is class shorter than 45 minutes? Highlight items most important to integration with core classroom studies and leave the rest for 'later'.

Steps

_____Start with a discussion on how to use the internet safely. Circle back on earlier conversations about internet neighborhood, how to be a good digital citizen. Go to today's virtual field trip and ask how they will stay safe in this digital neighborhood.

_____Ask one student to show on SmartScreen how to get to class internet start page where field trip link is (click link for an example of my start page). Help if they get stuck. I've found by this point in year, students are adept at this task.

_____Explain that today, students will take a virtual field trip to the same place they will physically visit next week (I'm using the Long Beach Aquarium as an example). Their job: Watch the videos listed on start page and help you make a list of which fish they want to learn more about/visit during the real field trip.

_____Play a video sharing Long Beach Aquarium. Make sure to enlarge to full screen and turn lights off (ask students how to do this). Here are some that worked well for me:

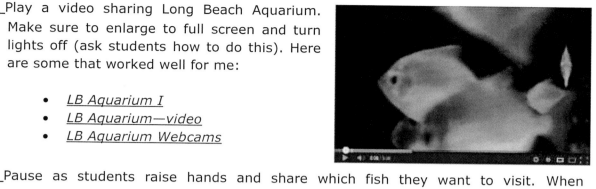

- *LB Aquarium I*
- *LB Aquarium—video*
- *LB Aquarium Webcams*

_____Pause as students raise hands and share which fish they want to visit. When completed, email list to class teacher.

_____Now show students how to find the location on Google Earth, using skills from Lesson 11. Using 'Directions', show how students will get to the destination from school. Together, explore the path they will travel, what they will see along the way, how long it will take, roadways they will travel.

_____Give students time to explore this route and the destination on their own (see inset for Google Earth image).

_____When done, students can revisit the virtual tour websites you shared with the class on their own computer or visit others you collected on the class internet start page.

_____As you teach, incorporate lesson vocabulary. Check this line if you did that today!

_____Continually throughout class, check for understanding. Expect students to solve problems and make decisions that follow class rules.

_____Close when completed. Tuck chairs under desk, headphones over tower; leave station as you found it.

_____Remind students to transfer knowledge to the classroom or home.

Assessment Strategies
- *Anecdotal*
- *Participated in class discussion*
- *Found and explored location on Google Earth*
- *Used skills learned in prior lessons to visit websites*

Trouble-shooting:
- *If students have difficulty dragging globe to move it, introduce arrow keys.*
- *You have print book and need website? Pick grade level and search (Alt+F) name on https://askatechteacher.wordpress.com/great-websites-for-kids/.*
- *Sometimes you need more than one week for a lesson. No worries. There are 32 lessons in text, 35ish in school year. Feel free to stretch a lesson a week or more.*

Extension:
- *Work in groups.*

- See if Street View guy will go inside the location (sometimes, he will, but not always).
- Have students practice keyboard skills with installed software or online site like Brown Bear (see appendix). Remind them of good posture, hands location and body position.
- Visit holiday websites like these (if you don't have a pdf, use 3-4 of your favorite sites):

  - Holiday Elf Games
  - Holiday match game
  - Holiday—Elf Academy
  - Design gingerbread house
  - NORAD Santa

- If this lesson doesn't work for your student group, use one from **How to Jumpstart the Inquiry-based Classroom.** It has 5 additional projects for Kindergarten (and all grades) aligned with the SL curriculum.

More Information:
- Lesson questions? Go to http://askatechteacher.com
- Kindergarten teaching wiki: http://smaatechk-3.wikispaces.com/This+Week+in+Tech—Kindergarten
- PDF: See appendix for bonus websites
- Follow keyboard lessons in K-8 Keyboard Curriculum (http://ow.ly/j6GH8)
- Full digital citizenship curriculum for kindergarten available here (http://www.structuredlearning.net/book/k-8-digital-citizenship-curriculum/)

If you don't get through everything, check completed items so you know what to get back to when you have time on later lessons. I find as I focus on the central idea of a lesson, clarifying questions sometimes take more time than I'd expect. I'm fine with that. There'll be lessons later that move faster than I planned.

> **"Pencil and paper: Archaic information storage and transmission device that works by depositing smears of graphite on bleached wood pulp. Requires operator skilled at so-called 'handwriting'."**
>
> **Anonymous**

Lesson #14—Devil is in the Details

Vocabulary	Problem solving	Big Idea
Detail Digital neighborhood Export Graphics Greeting Open House Screen capture Screen shot Slideshow Surroundings	Can't exit program (try Alt+F4) Screen froze (click program on taskbar) Can't open program (push enter) Why do I curve my fingers when I keyboard? (That gives them room to stretch to more keys—like springs) I didn't get all the details into my picture (that's OK) I got off my website (click tab or back button)	*Pay attention to your surroundings.*
Time Required *45 minutes*	**NETS-S Standards** *3a, 4b*	**CCSS** *CCSS.ELA-Literacy.SL.K*

Essential Question
How do visual details convey information that helps with decisions?

Overview

Materials

Internet, sample picture, drawing program, enrichment web sites, printer, iPads (if using these), keyboarding program

Teacher Preparation

- Talk with classroom teacher to find out what picture supports inquiry.
- Have websites on class start page to support inquiry unit
- Is class shorter than 45 minutes? Highlight items most important to your integration with core classroom studies and leave the rest for 'later'

Steps

_____Discuss 'details' with students. What does the statement, "They can't see the forest for the trees" mean? How about 'Devil is in the details"?

_____Point to something in the classroom and ask students what they see. Dig deeper with each student to find all the details that make up a bulletin board, a wall sign, a computer station, or whatever works for you.

_____Open a drawing program like KidPix, TuxPaint, Paint, or Kerpoof. Do this as independently as possible. Open yours on class SmartScreen.

_____Draw a shape, say, a house, to get students

started. Draw only outline. Have students draw with you.

_____Ask students to suggest a detail that goes into the house, i.e., a front door. Remind students of the rules the class agreed-upon for discussions (e.g., listening to others and taking turns speaking).

_____Draw the front door and have students draw one on their canvas.

_____Ask for another detail and draw that one as students add it to their canvas.

_____Continue until students run out of details (or you run out of time).

_____Add student name and a greeting.

_____Have students print and export. Assist as needed. Remind them this drawing will be part of their Open House slideshow (What's Open House?).

_____When done, practice keyboarding on installed software or online website for 10 minutes. Students are still working on key placement, not speed and/or accuracy.

_____When done, go to class start page where you have websites that tie into class inquiry or holiday theme. Demonstrate sites.

_____Before students go to websites, remind them of internet safety.

_____Continually throughout class, check for understanding. Expect students to solve problems as they maneuver through lesson and make decisions that follow class rules.

_____As you teach, incorporate lesson vocabulary. Check this line if you did that today!

_____Remind students to transfer knowledge to class or home.

_____Tuck chairs under desk, headphones over tower; leave station as it was.

Assessment of Learning

- *Anecdotal observation*
- *Followed directions*
- *Understood how details make up the whole*
- *Completed project*
- *Joined class conversations*
- *Began to show knowledge of key placement*

Trouble-shooting:

- *Occasionally when students have difficulty doing what you are teaching, ask why. And listen. You may be surprised by the answer.*
- *If this takes too long, add less details. You will still make your point.*
- *Drawing program won't allow saving? Take a screen shot and save that (using Jing, Snippet, or similar).*
- *You have print book and need website? Pick grade level and search (Alt+F) name on https://askatechteacher.wordpress.com/great-websites-for-kids/.*
- *Sometimes you need more than one week for a lesson. No worries. There are 32 in text, 35ish in school year. Feel free to stretch a lesson a week or more.*

Extension:

- *Draw picture using an iPad app.*
- *Do it backwards: Draw picture and ask students to describe details that created it.*
- *Replace this lesson with Kindergarten lesson #1—Blabberize Me! in curriculum extendors (http://www.structuredlearning.net/book/k-6-curriculum-extender/).*

- *Instead of drawing a picture, ask students to follow a series of directions on SmartScreen. They can move at their own pace. This is a good activity to extend Lesson to a second week.*

More Information:
- *Lesson questions? Go to http://askatechteacher.com*
- *Kindergarten teaching wiki: http://smaatechk-3.wikispaces.com/This+Week+in+Tech—Kindergarten*
- *PDF: See appendix for bonus websites*
- *Follow keyboard lessons in K-8 Keyboard Curriculum (http://ow.ly/j6GH8)*

If you don't get through everything, check completed items so you know what to get back to when you have time on later lessons. I find as I focus on the central idea of a lesson, clarifying questions sometimes take more time than I'd expect. I'm fine with that. There'll be lessons later that move faster than I planned.

**Computer:
a device designed to speed and automate errors.**

Lesson #15—Open House: Me I

Vocabulary	Problem solving	Big Idea
Caps lock Cursor Dragging Export Grammar Icon Mouse buttons Multimedia Open House Palette Shift key Slideshow Toolbar Tools Undo (Oops guy)	My monitor doesn't work (wake up mouse, check power) My computer doesn't work (check power, check plug) My volume doesn't work (check headphones connection) My mouse doesn't work right (is it upside down?) Why can't I save? Shift doesn't work (caps lock on?) Where's the period? What's the difference between backspace and delete? I can't double click (push enter)	*Communicating ideas requires a combination of media*
Time Required *45 minutes*	**NETS-S Standards** *1a, 2b*	**CCSS** *CCSS.ELA-Literacy.W.K.2*

Essential Question
How does a combination of drawing and writing share information text can't?

Overview

Materials

Internet, drawing program, keyboard program, updated start page, mouse websites

Teacher Preparation

- What topic is being discussed in classroom? Have 4-5 websites available on class internet start page that tie into those conversations.
- Is class shorter than 45 minutes? Highlight items most important to your integration with core classroom studies and leave the rest for 'later'.

Steps

_____Warm up with keyboarding either on installed software or an internet site like Brown Bear Typing:

- *Curve fingers over home row*
- *Use good posture—legs in front of body*
- *Keep keyboard in front of body, mouse to right (or left if needed)*
- *Keep feet flat on floor, not under bottom*

_____This project starts a four-drawing series that students will prepare for Open House (you might need to take time to discuss the meaning of 'Open House'). Students will

x type anything special about yourself

tell a story of themselves to celebrate tech skills accomplished during kindergarten. They will use all the basics (tools, toolbars, fills, drag-and-drop, backgrounds, clipart, text and everything else you covered throughout the year). All four will be ready by Open House. This is the first and uses pencil tool and toolbars. Be prepared to allow one week to practice, one to export if necessary.

_____Open drawing software (i.e., KidPix, Paint, TuxPaint, Kerpoof, or other). We use KidPix for this example.

_____Use pencil tool to draw and 5 colors from palette.

_____Use ABC tool, caps lock, font size 72, to write a sentence "J is for Jenny (using their first initial and name)" or other sentence to introduce student (see examples at end of lesson). This is first slideshow slide.

_____Most students need to edit their sentence. Explain how to edit (place cursor where mistake is and backspace or delete—what's the difference).

_____Drag and drop letters in name onto page. Give students time to play with the fun animations.

_____Observe students as they work to be sure they hold the mouse correctly (palm at bottom, pointer and middle fingers on buttons, thumb on side). If necessary, circle back on mouse websites from earlier lessons to reinforce skills like click, drag-and-drop, and hover.

_____Don't worry about finishing—we won't export today.

_____Close down to desktop. Tuck chairs under desk, headphones over tower; leave station as you found it.

_____As you teach, incorporate lesson vocabulary. Check this line if you did that today!

_____Continually throughout class, check for understanding. Expect students to solve problems and make decisions that follow class rules.

_____Remind students to transfer knowledge to classroom or home.

Assessment Strategies
- *Anecdotal*
- *Understood how pictures and text collaborate to deliver a message*
- *Displayed keyboarding skills*
- *Used mouse correctly*
- *Remembered and used skills already learned*

Trouble-shooting:
- *You have print book and need website? Pick grade level and search (Alt+F) name on https://askatechteacher.wordpress.com/great-websites-for-kids/.*
- *Student can't finish? It doesn't matter to the goals of this project. If they're working on tools, toolbars, mouse skills, they're succeeding!*
- *Student can't fit their name in the space? Discuss planning and layout with students. If they're taking two weeks on this project, suggest how to make changes next week.*

Extension:

- Add up to 5 stamps that share student interests.
- Add one text detail about student. This can be in response to a prompt from the teacher, i.e., 'What is your favorite activity?'
- Don't use caps lock. Expect student to use shift key to capitalize as needed and add a period to end of sentence. Discuss 'grammar' with students.
- Some students finish early? Provide mouse websites on class internet start page that reinforce mouse skills or websites that tie into class inquiry.
- If this lesson doesn't work for your student group, use one from **_How to Jumpstart the Inquiry-based Classroom._** It has 5 additional projects for Kindergarten (and all grades) aligned with the SL curriculum.

More Information:

- Lesson questions? Go to http://askatechteacher.com
- Kindergarten teaching wiki: http://smaatechk-3.wikispaces.com/This+Week+in+Tech—Kindergarten
- PDF: See appendix for bonus websites
- Follow keyboard lessons in K-8 Keyboard Curriculum (http://ow.ly/j6GH8)

If you don't get through everything, check completed items so you know what to get back to when you have time on later lessons. I find as I focus on the central idea of a lesson, clarifying questions sometimes take more time than I'd expect. I'm fine with that. There'll be lessons later that move faster than I planned.

Lesson #16—Open House: Me II

Vocabulary	Problem solving	Big Idea
Cursor Desktop Drag Edit Export Icon Mouse buttons Multimedia Open House Palette Slideshow Space bar Toolbar Tools Undo (Oops guy)	How do I capitalize (use caps lock for all letters and shift key for one) My capital won't go off (is caps lock on?) What's the difference between backspace and delete? How do I edit (put cursor where you want to edit) My mouse isn't working right (is it upside down?) I need two hands for mouse (probably not) I can't find the dog alphabet (nested toolbar)	*Communicating ideas requires a combination of media*
Time Required *45 minutes*	**NETS-S Standards** *1a, 2b*	**CCSS** *CCSS.ELA-Literacy.W.K.2*

Essential Question
How does a combination of drawing and writing share information text can't?

Overview

Materials

Internet, drawing program, keyboard program, updated class internet start page, mouse websites, printer

Teacher Preparation
- Have mouse websites on class internet start page for students who need extra help
- What topic is being discussed in the classroom? Have 4-5 websites available on internet start page that tie into those discussions.
- Is class shorter than 45 minutes? Highlight items most important to your integration with core classroom studies and leave the rest for 'later'.

Steps

_____This is the 2nd week on 1st drawing for Open House slideshow sharing the range of skills kindergartners learn in technology. Two weeks for each drawing allows one week to practice, one to export (to jpg). This is a great way to reinforce new skills.

_____Open drawing software (i.e., KidPix, Paint, TuxPaint, Kerpoof, or other). We use KidPix in this example.

_____Use pencil tool to draw yourself. Use medium to thick from toolbar. Use 5 colors from color palette.

_____Observe students as they work to be sure they hold mouse correctly (palm at bottom, pointer and middle fingers on buttons, thumb on side). If necessary, circle back on mouse websites from earlier lessons to reinforce skills like click, drag-and-drop, and hover.

_____Use ABC text tool, caps lock, font size 72, to write a sentence "J is for Jenny (using their first initial and name)" or another sentence to introduce student (see samples at end of lesson). This will be the first slide in slideshow.

_____Most students need to edit their sentence. Explain how to edit (place cursor where you want it and backspace or delete—what's the difference?).

_____Use animation tool, alphabet toolbar. Drag and drop letters of student name onto page. Give time to play with these fun animations.

_____Students should be comfortable with this lesson because they practiced last week. Remind how to edit their sentence in case they make a mistake. Show the difference between backspace and delete. See poster at end of this lesson.

_____Export with help (what's the difference from 'save'?) Don't print—this is a surprise for parents! Students can print at Open House.

_____Those who finish: Practice keyboarding either on installed software or an internet site like Brown Bear Typing:

- *Use good posture—legs in front of body*
- *Keep keyboard in front of body, mouse to the right (or left if needed)*
- *Focus on remembering where keys are—nothing else*

Assessment Strategies
- *Anecdotal*
- *Understood how pictures and text collaborate to deliver a message*
- *Exported project*
- *Remembered skills from prior week*
- *Used correct keyboarding and mouse skills*

_____Close down to desktop. Tuck chairs under desk, headphones over tower; leave station as it was.

_____As you teach, incorporate lesson vocabulary. Check this line if you did that today!

_____Continually throughout class, check for understanding. Expect students to solve problems and make decisions that follow class rules.

_____Remind students to transfer knowledge to classroom or home.

Trouble-shooting:
- *Running out of time? Write name with text tool.*

- *Students aren't holding mouse correctly? Have them visit mouse websites if there is time at end of class.*
- *Drawing program won't allow saving? Take a screen shot and save that (using Jing, Snippet, or similar).*
- *Students turn monitors off so they don't have to figure out how to close down programs? Have students leave monitors on at end of class.*
- *You have print book and need website? Pick grade level and search (Alt+F) name on https://askatechteacher.wordpress.com/great-websites-for-kids/.*

Extension:
- *Add up to 5 stamps that share student interests.*
- *Add one text detail about student. This can be in response to a prompt from the teacher, i.e., 'What is your favorite activity?'*
- *Instead of caps lock, use shift key to capitalize as needed (see inset).*
- *Use this second week as a formative assessment. What do students remember of skills practiced last week?*
- *If this lesson doesn't work for your student group, use one from **How to Jumpstart the Inquiry-based Classroom.** It has 5 additional projects for Kindergarten (and all grades) aligned with the SL curriculum.*

More Information:
- *Lesson questions? Go to http://askatechteacher.com*
- *Kindergarten teaching wiki:*
  http://smaatechk-3.wikispaces.com/This+Week+in+Tech—Kindergarten
- *PDF: See appendix for bonus websites*
- *Follow keyboard lessons in K-8 Keyboard Curriculum (http://ow.ly/j6GH8)*

If you don't get through everything, check completed items so you know what to get back to when you have time on later lessons. I find as I focus on the central idea of a lesson, clarifying questions sometimes take more time than I'd expect. I'm fine with that. There'll be lessons later that move faster than I planned.

TWO WAYS TO EDIT

BACKSPACE

DELETE

Deletes to the left, one character at a time

Deletes to the right, one character at a time

Lesson #17—Site Words

Vocabulary	Problem solving	Big Idea
Clipart *Digital neighborhood* *Dolch words* *Edit* *Export* *Grammar* *Punctuation* *Site words* *Stamps* *Toolbar*	*How do I close a program (file-exit or the X)* *My program disappeared (check taskbar)* *My capitals don't work (is caps lock on?)* *What's the difference between backspace and delete?* *Why do I export rather than save?*	*Use images and text to demonstrate understanding of words used in conversation.*
Time Required *30 minutes*	**NETS-S Standards** *4d, 6d*	**CCSS** *CCSS.ELA-Literacy.L.K.6*

Essential Question
Does an idea have to be communicated with text or can I use pictures?

Overview

Materials

Internet, drawing program, printer, site word list, keyboarding program, websites that connect to class inquiry

Teacher Preparation

- Get site words from class teacher. Have her send them to you weekly so you can connect whenever there is time
- Is class shorter than 45 minutes? Highlight items most important to your integration with core classroom studies and leave the rest for 'later'

Steps

_____Display site words on SmartScreen. Say them together. Brainstorm what type of pictures would support each word.

_____Open drawing program (KidPix, TuxPaint, Kerpoof, Pixie, Paint, other). We use KidPix.

_____Demonstrate how to construct a sentence using pictures and their class site words to convey a message.

_____Have students select three or four site words. Using text tool, font size 48, create a quasi-sentence. If relevant, leave space where required for picture (see inset).

_____Fill in words with stamps or clipart.

_____Remind students how to edit sentences (see poster at end of Lesson 16): Backspace edits to left, delete edits to right.

_____Have students print independently; ask for assistance if needed.

_____Export (rather than save so they can use picture in end-of-year slideshow) with assistance.

_____Done? Practice keyboarding with installed software or online site. Remind students to use correct posture, correct hand position.

_____As you teach, incorporate lesson vocabulary. Check this line if you did that today!

_____Continually throughout class, check for understanding. Expect students to solve problems and make decisions that follow class rules.

_____Remind students to transfer knowledge to classroom or home.

_____Tuck chairs under desk, headphones over tower; leave station as you found it.

Assessment Strategies

- *Anecdotal*
- *Completed project*
- *Demonstrated command of standard English (where relevant)*
- *Remembered skills from prior lessons*

Trouble-shooting:

- *Drawing program won't allow saving? Take a screen shot and save (using Jing, Snippet, or similar).*
- *You have print book and need website? Pick grade level and search (Alt+F) name on https://askatechteacher.wordpress.com/great-websites-for-kids/.*
- *Sometimes you need more than one week for a lesson. No worries. There are 32 lessons in text, 35ish in the school year. Feel free to stretch a lesson a week or more.*

Extension:

- *Add a border to decorate project (see example at end of lesson).*
- *Include grammar conventions being covered in class (i.e., don't use caps lock).*
- *If you don't have access to site words, use Dolch words. These are the 220 most commonly used vocabulary in children's books. Words on next pages are from Kindergarten list.*
- *Revisit this project throughout the year as students study site words.*
- *More time? Have a list of websites that tie into class inquiry on internet start page. Introduce these by reviewing how to safely traverse the internet neighborhood*
- *If this lesson doesn't work for your student group, use one from **How to Jumpstart the Inquiry-based Classroom.** It has 5 additional projects for Kindergarten (and all grades) aligned with the SL curriculum.*

More Information:

- *Lesson questions? Go to http://askatechteacher.com*
- *Kindergarten teaching wiki: http://smaatechk-3.wikispaces.com/This+Week+in+Tech—Kindergarten*
- *PDF: See appendix for bonus websites.*
- *Follow keyboard lessons in K-8 Keyboard Curriculum (http://ow.ly/j6GH8)*
- *Full digital citizenship curriculum for kindergarten available here (http://www.structuredlearning.net/book/k-8-digital-citizenship-curriculum/)*

If you don't get through everything, check completed items so you know what to get back to when you have time on later lessons. I find as I focus on the central idea of a lesson, clarifying questions sometimes take more time than I'd expect. I'm fine with that. There'll be lessons later that move faster than I planned.

Kindergarten Dolch Words

a	come	he	not	two
all	can	I	now	up
am	come	if	on	want
an	did	in	one	was
and	do	is	of	well
any	find	it	put	went
as	for	jump	ran	we
ask	four	let	red	were
at	get	like	ride	white
are	girl	little	run	will
be	go	look	said	with
big	had	make	say	yes
black	have	may	see	yellow
blue	has	me	she	you
boy	her	my	so	
brown	his	must	take	
but	him	no	the	
by	how	not	to	

Lesson #18—Open House: My Family

Vocabulary	Problem solving	Big Idea
Caps lock *Click* *Drag-and-drop* *Drop down menu* *Export* *Icon* *Keyboarding* *Save* *Screen shot* *Shift* *Text tool* *Tool* *Toolbar*	*I can't exit (Alt+F4)* *What's the difference between export and save?* *My shift key doesn't work (is caps lock on?)* *I can't find alphabet under dog (click drop down list)* *I goofed (use Oops guy or paint over it)* *This is hard (that's why we practice)* *I can't fit title on page (plan ahead)*	***Communicating ideas requires a combination of media***
Time Required *45 minutes*	**NETS-S Standards** *1a, 2b*	**CCSS** *CCSS.ELA-Literacy.W.K.2*

Essential Question
How do images catch viewer attention where text can't?

Overview

Materials

Internet, drawing program, keyboard program, mouse websites (if needed), websites that tie into classroom inquiry

Teacher Preparation

- Know what is being discussed in class and tie into it with extra websites
- Is class shorter than 45 minutes? Highlight items most important to your integration with core classroom studies and leave the rest for 'later'.

Steps

_____Students review basics (tools, toolbars, fills, drag-drop, backgrounds, clipart) by creating 4 pictures in a drawing program. All four will be ready by Open House. This is the second drawing and teaches paint brush, toolbars, and reinforces drag-and-drop.

_____Remind students about Open House each time they create a drawing.

_____Open drawing program (KidPix, Pixie, Kerpoof, TuxPaint, Paint or other). We use KidPix for this sample. Demonstrate on SmartScreen how to complete this project:

- *Use animation (dog) or text toolbar, to write 'My Family'.*
- *Use paint brush tool to draw family. Use a different brush for each family member. Use at least 5 colors*

_____Do students notice how the drawings communicate much more than the words. What do students know about the family based on the drawing?

_____If necessary, remind students of agreed-upon rules for class conversations.

_____After discussing, have students practice. Remind them to use drag-and-drop mouse skills for letters and left click-drag for paint brush.

_____Observe students as they work to be sure they hold the mouse correctly (palm at bottom, point and middle finger on buttons, thumb on side) and use drag skills to paint. If necessary, circle back on mouse websites covered in earlier lessons to reinforce skills like click, drag-and-drop, hover.

_____Because these tools are familiar (paint brush and dog alphabet), students may be ready to export rather than wait until next week. If not, extend this lesson one more week.

_____As you teach, incorporate lesson. Check this line if you did that today!

_____Continually throughout class, check for understanding. Expect students to solve problems and make decisions that follow class rules.

_____Done? Practice keyboarding on installed software or online typing site:

- *Curve hands over home row*
- *Use good posture*
- *Keep keyboard in front of body, mouse to the right (or left if needed)*
- *Keep feet in front of body, not under bottom*

Assessment Strategies
- *Anecdotal*
- *Undestood that both words and images deliver a message*
- *Used all skills*
- *Exported to network*
- *Used keyboarding skills*
- *Joined class conversation*

_____Close to desktop.

_____Remind students to transfer knowledge to the classroom or home.

_____Tuck chairs under desk, headphones over tower; leave station as it was.

Trouble-shooting:
- *Occasionally when students have difficulty doing what you are teaching, ask why. And listen. You may be surprised by the answer.*
- *Students run out of room for title? Encourage them to drag letters to left to provide more room. Better yet: Before they start, think through layout. Where should they put the first letter so there is enough room for both words?*
- *Drawing program won't allow saving? Take a screen shot and save that (using Jing, Snippet, or similar).*

- You have print book and need website? Pick grade level and search (Alt+F) name on https://askatechteacher.wordpress.com/great-websites-for-kids/.

Extension:
- Use ABC text tool to add names of family members (see inset).
- Practice mouse skills on websites (for those who need it).
- Visit websites on start page that tie into class inquiry.
- If this lesson doesn't work for your student group, use one from **How to Jumpstart the Inquiry-based Classroom.** It has 5 additional projects for Kindergarten (and all grades) aligned with the SL curriculum.

More Information:
- Lesson questions? Go to http://askatechteacher.com
- Kindergarten teaching wiki: http://smaatechk-3.wikispaces.com/This+Week+in+Tech—Kindergarten
- PDF: See appendix for bonus websites
- Follow keyboard lessons in K-8 Keyboard Curriculum (http://ow.ly/j6GH8)

If you don't get through everything, check completed items so you know what to get back to when you have time on later lessons. I find as I focus on the central idea of a lesson, clarifying questions sometimes take more time than I'd expect. I'm fine with that. There'll be lessons later that move faster than I planned.

Lesson #19—Coloring Book and Fills I

Vocabulary	Problem solving	Big Idea
Background tool	How to save (Ctrl+S)	Colors selected for a picture make a big difference in how the story is told
Canvas	How to print (Ctrl+P)	
Coloring book	How to open a program (double click program icon)	
Desktop		
Drag and drop	My fill flowed into another section (close section)	
Fill	I used the wrong fill (Use Ooops guy)	
Icon		
Paint bucket	Oops guy doesn't work (that's OK. That's why we practice)	
Texture		
Tool bar		
Time Required *45 minutes*	**NETS-S Standards** *1a, 2b*	**CCSS** *CCSS.ELA-Literacy.W.K.6*

Essential Question
How can I reinforce what I want to say?

Overview

Materials

Internet, drawing program with a 'coloring book' or online coloring pages, printer, keyboarding program

Teacher Preparation

- Find coloring pages that align with topics being discussed in classroom. Upload to a site students can access through the drawing program used in your school
- Is class period shorter than 45 minutes? Highlight the items most important to your integration with core classroom studies and leave the rest for 'later'.

Steps

_____Warm up with keyboarding using installed software or online typing site. As students practice, remind them to use good posture, both hands on keyboard, elbows at sides.

_____Close after about ten minutes.

_____Today, students will use the drawing program (KidPix, Pixie, Paint, or an online website). They'll practice paint buckets and fills using the familiar coloring book concept. Instead of crayons, students use buckets.

_____As this is a new skill, allow one week to practice, one to export/print.

_____Discuss coloring books with students. How do students use them? They have a picture divided into sections and the student colors each section—right?

_____This can be done on the computer, too.

_____It starts with 'fill' tool on toolbar. Explain the purpose of fills.

_____Students will make three drawings, one using each paint bucket (if not using KidPix, it may not be three different buckets). They will notice the difference in how a message is communicated in their drawing with different fills: 1) fill has one color, different textures (see first inset), 2) fill has many wild colors, seemingly unrelated (see second inset), and 3) fill has realistic fills (see third inset).

_____Model using a drawing program used at your school or a holiday coloring page from internet from a site such as this (http://www.coloring-book.info/coloring/). Here, I'll use KidPix Backgrounds—Color me.

_____Students open KidPix.

_____Go to background tool on toolbar; select 'color me' backgrounds.

_____Try several by dragging-and-dropping to canvas. Select one.

_____Select first paint bucket, then select a color from pallet. Students will use that one color and many textures (from lower tool bar) throughout (see first inset). Demonstrate how they pick a texture and pour into one section of picture, then continue picking different textures until picture is 'colored'.

_____Use second paint bucket for a pizzazz picture filled with rainbow color (see second inset).

_____Don't worry about finishing—we'll get to third bucket next week.

_____As you teach, incorporate lesson vocabulary. Check this line if you did that today!

_____Continually throughout class, check for understanding. Expect students to solve problems as they maneuver through lesson and make decisions that follow class rules.

_____Exit program. Tuck chairs under desk, headphones over tower; leave station as you found it.

_____Remind students to transfer knowledge to classroom or home.

Assessment Strategies
- Anecdotal
- Understood how digital tools help deliver a message to various audiences
- Used prior knowledge
- Followed directions

Trouble-shooting:

- *Drawing program doesn't have this sort of coloring book? Adapt to fit what's available. The lesson's big idea is:* **Colors selected for a picture make a big difference in how the story is told**. *Work your program to deliver that message.*
- *You have print book and need website? Pick grade level and search (Alt+F) name on https://askatechteacher.wordpress.com/great-websites-for-kids/.*

Extension:

- *If you use online coloring pages, discuss internet safety before students access site*
- *If you use online coloring book site, discuss copyright protections for materials.*
- *Some students finish early? Provide websites on class internet start page that tie into class inquiry.*
- *If this lesson doesn't work for your student group, use one from* **How to Jumpstart the Inquiry-based Classroom.** *It has 5 additional projects for Kindergarten (and all grades) aligned with the SL curriculum.*

More Information:

- *Lesson questions? Go to http://askatechteacher.com*
- *Kindergarten teaching wiki: http://smaatechk-3.wikispaces.com/This+Week+in+Tech—Kindergarten*
- *PDF: See appendix for bonus websites*
- *Follow keyboard lessons in K-8 Keyboard Curriculum (http://ow.ly/j6GH8)*

If you don't get through everything, check completed items so you know what to get back to when you have time on later lessons. I find as I focus on the central idea of a lesson, clarifying questions sometimes take more time than I'd expect. I'm fine with that. There'll be lessons later that move faster than I planned.

> ## Do not touch MY iPad. It's not an usPad. It's not a wePad. It's not an ourPad. It's an iPad.
>
> ## —Anonymous

Lesson #20—Coloring Book and Fills II

Vocabulary	Problem solving	Big Idea
Desktop	How do I change colors (select palette and color)	*Colors selected for a picture make a big difference in how the story is told*
Digital tools	Can't find icon (use Start button)	
Export	How do I print (file-print)	
Fill	TTLJr won't type (is caps lock on?)	
Icon	I can't close the file (Alt+F4)	
Oops guy	Why can't I use headphones (they're distracting)	
Paint bucket		
Slideshow	My computer won't work (check power)	
Start button	I saved instead of exported (open file from network folder and export)	
Text tool		
Texture	My fill doesn't work (you've already added one fill—you can't add another)	
Toolbars		
Tools		

Time Required	NETS-S Standards	CCSS
45 minutes	*1a, 2b*	*CCSS.ELA-Literacy.W.K.6*

Essential Question
How can I reinforce what I want to say?

Overview

Materials

Internet, drawing program with a 'coloring book' or online coloring pages, printer, keyboarding program

Teacher Preparation

- Find coloring pages that align with topics being discussed in classroom. Upload to a location (i.e., class server) students can access through school's drawing program
- Is class shorter than 45 minutes? Highlight the items most important to your integration with core classroom studies and leave the rest for 'later'.

Steps

_____Today, students finish coloring book project. Remind them they colored a picture using the paint buckets. Show samples from last week of first and second paint bucket drawings—1) with one color and different textures (see first inset), 2) with wild unrelated colors (see second inset). Think about what each of these communicated. Which said the most about what student felt?

_____This week, students will make the third drawing—realistic colors—then pick one of the three drawings—that best communicated their ideas—and recreate it.

_____Open KidPix (or TuxPaint or other drawing program used in your school).

_____Go to background tool; select 'color me' backgrounds with limited assistance.

_____Drag and drop one—maybe the one student worked with last week. If using a coloring page from an online site, add it as an image.

_____Use third paint bucket to color picture. This time, students make it as realistic as possible by using fills that fit (see third inset). Demonstrate on SmartScreen by showing what can be used for sky, ground, etc. (see inset).

_____Be careful—once a fill is added, it can't be filled over. Use the Oops guy—but he only goes back one step!

_____Have students practice this third fill, then discuss. What did they feel when they 1) used only one color, 2) used rainbow colors, 3) used realistic colors? Which felt right for them?

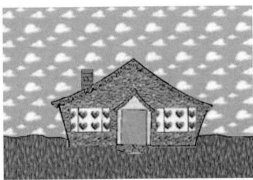

_____Now recreate whichever they liked best. Use ABC text tool to add their name.

_____Print when finished. Export for Open House slideshow.

_____As you teach, incorporate lesson vocabulary. Check this line if you did that!

_____Continually throughout class, check for understanding. Expect students to solve problems and make decisions that follow class rules.

_____Those who finish, practice keyboarding with installed software or online typing website

_____Remind students to transfer knowledge to classroom or home.

_____Tuck chairs under desk, headphones over tower; leave station as you found it.

Assessment Strategies

- *Anecdotal*
- *Use skills from earlier lessons*
- *Understand how digital tools communicate*
- *Project completion*
- *Join class conversation*

Trouble-shooting:

- *Drawing program won't allow saving? Take a screen shot and save that (using Jing, Snippet, or similar).*
- *You have print book and need website? Pick grade level and search (Alt+F) name on https://askatechteacher.wordpress.com/great-websites-for-kids/.*
- *Sometimes you need more than one week for a lesson. No worries. There are 32 lessons in text, 35ish in the school year. Feel free to stretch a lesson a week or more.*

Extension:

- *Have students go to a website with coloring pages and pick one that ties in with class inquiry. Introduce this option by reminding students how to stay safe on the internet.*
- *Use this second week as a formative assessment. What skills do students remember from last week?*
- *If this lesson doesn't work for your student group, use one from **How to Jumpstart the Inquiry-based Classroom.** It has 5 additional projects for Kindergarten (and all grades) aligned with the SL curriculum.*

More Information:

- *Lesson questions? Go to http://askatechteacher.com*
- *Kindergarten teaching wiki:*
  http://smaatechk-3.wikispaces.com/This+Week+in+Tech—Kindergarten
- *PDF: See appendix for bonus websites*
- *Follow keyboard lessons in K-8 Keyboard Curriculum (http://ow.ly/j6GH8)*

If you don't get through everything, check completed items so you know what to get back to when you have time on later lessons. I find as I focus on the central idea of a lesson, clarifying questions sometimes take more time than I'd expect. I'm fine with that. There'll be lessons later that move faster than I planned.

> **Education is the most powerful weapon which you can use to change the world.**
>
> **—Nelson Mandela**

Lesson #21—Valentine Card

Vocabulary	Problem solving	Big Idea
Border Double click Enter key Export Fill Font size Greeting Palette Start button Text tool Toolbar	I can't find my file folder (are you logged in correctly?) I can't find program (check Start button) My double-click doesn't work (use enter) Where's the enter key Where'd my paint brush go (in KidPix)? (Be sure you're on purple splotch)	*I can share my excitement with pictures and words via digital tools*

Time Required	NETS-S Standards	CCSS
45 minutes	*1b, 2b*	*CCSS.ELA-Literacy.W.K.6*

Essential Question
How do I use digital tools to produce and publish my writing?

Overview

Materials

Internet, drawing program, printer, share location

Teacher Preparation
- Know what class has discussed about Valentine's Day
- Have a digital gallery (via a class blog or wiki) to share student Valentine greetings
- Is class shorter than 45 minutes? Highlight items most important to your integration with core classroom studies and leave the rest for 'later'.

Steps

_____Have students open drawing program (KidPix, TuxPaint, Pixie, Paint, or other) as independently as possible. We use KidPix in this example.

_____Today, they'll make a Valentine Card for family/friends. They'll use paint bucket backgrounds (as practiced in prior lessons), spray can, paint brush, text tool.

_____Show a sample on the SmartScreen and ask a student to come up and show in the school drawing program where each of the parts came from:

- *Paint brush*
- *Paint bucket*
- *Text*

- *Backgrounds*
- *Spray can (this is probably new, but some students have the program at home and will happily share their knowledge)*

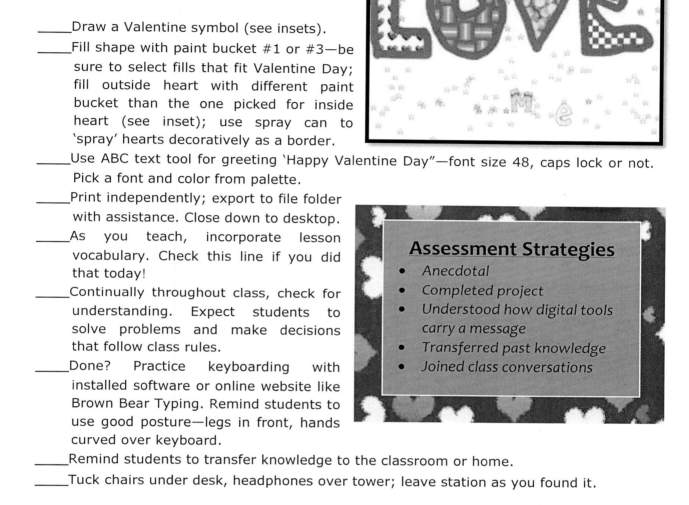

_____Draw a Valentine symbol (see insets).

_____Fill shape with paint bucket #1 or #3—be sure to select fills that fit Valentine Day; fill outside heart with different paint bucket than the one picked for inside heart (see inset); use spray can to 'spray' hearts decoratively as a border.

_____Use ABC text tool for greeting 'Happy Valentine Day"—font size 48, caps lock or not. Pick a font and color from palette.

_____Print independently; export to file folder with assistance. Close down to desktop.

_____As you teach, incorporate lesson vocabulary. Check this line if you did that today!

_____Continually throughout class, check for understanding. Expect students to solve problems and make decisions that follow class rules.

_____Done? Practice keyboarding with installed software or online website like Brown Bear Typing. Remind students to use good posture—legs in front, hands curved over keyboard.

_____Remind students to transfer knowledge to the classroom or home.

_____Tuck chairs under desk, headphones over tower; leave station as you found it.

Assessment Strategies
- *Anecdotal*
- *Completed project*
- *Understood how digital tools carry a message*
- *Transferred past knowledge*
- *Joined class conversations*

Trouble-shooting:
- *Leave out the 's in 'Valentine's'. It's difficult for kindergartners.*
- *Drawing program won't allow saving? Take a screen shot and save that (using Jing, Snippet, or similar).*
- *You have print book and need website? Pick grade level and search (Alt+F) name on* https://askatechteacher.wordpress.com/great-websites-for-kids/.
- *Sometimes you need more than one week for a lesson. No worries. There are 32 lessons in text, 35ish in school year. Feel free to stretch a lesson a week or more.*

Extension:
- *Collect greetings into an online portfolio that students can share with parents (class blog, wiki, or other).*
- *Greeting cards are a great way to review student skills with a project they love. Use this as a student-directed authentic project whenever a holiday comes up.*

- *If this lesson doesn't work for your student group, use one from **How to Jumpstart the Inquiry-based Classroom.** It has 5 additional projects for Kindergarten (and all grades) aligned with the SL curriculum.*

More Information:
- *Lesson questions? Go to http://askatechteacher.com*
- *Kindergarten teaching wiki: http://smaatechk-3.wikispaces.com/This+Week+in+Tech—Kindergarten*
- *PDF: See appendix for bonus websites*
- *Follow keyboard lessons in K-8 Keyboard Curriculum (http://ow.ly/j6GH8)*

If you don't get through everything, check completed items so you know what to get back to when you have time on later lessons. I find as I focus on the central idea of a lesson, clarifying questions sometimes take more time than I'd expect. I'm fine with that. There'll be lessons later that move faster than I planned.

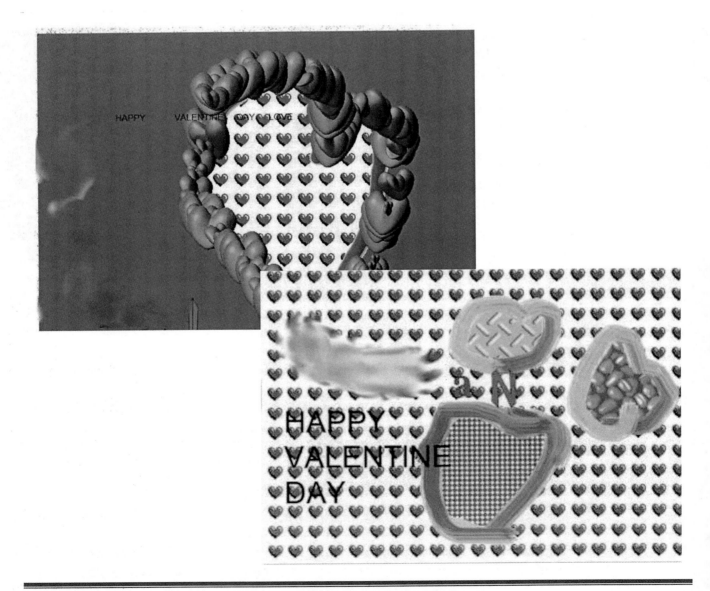

Lesson #22—Open House: My House I

Vocabulary	Problem solving	Big Idea
Click Desktop Drag-and-drop Export Icon Monitor Mouse buttons Paint brush Palette Toolbars Tools	How do I print (file-print) How do I save (file-save) I can't open the program from icon (push enter) I can't find start button (push flying windows) What's the difference between save and export? My trees are the wrong color—in KidPix (change color palette)	*I can share information about a topic through drawings*
Time Required 45 minutes	**NETS-S Standards** 1c, 6b	**CCSS** CCSS.ELA-Literacy.W.K

Essential Question
How can I use drawings to convey information about a topic?

Overview

Materials

Internet, drawing program, keyboard program, mouse websites

Teacher Preparation

- Have mouse websites on class internet start page for those who need them
- Is class shorter than 45 minutes? Highlight items most important to your integration with core classroom studies and leave the rest for 'later'.

Steps

_____This is the third picture students create using art to supply detail about a topic (construction of a house—what is included). They also share the range of technology skills learned in kindergarten. Practice this week, export next. These tools focus on mouse skills like drag-and-drop and clicking.

_____Demonstrate how to draw a house with KidPix tools on class SmartScreen. What is included in a house? As students mention detail, add to sample on screen. Walls? Door? Windows? Roof? Use only construction tools like bricks, boards, windows, doors, roof. See inset (which includes landscaping—this is extra).

_____Use animation alphabet tool to write 'My House'. Ask students to spell these two words as you write them.

_____Now students open KidPix (or other drawing program like TuxPaint, Kerpoof, Pixie, Paint) and create their picture.

_____Let them know they won't save this week. This is just practice.

_____Notice if students have difficulty with mouse skills. Are they holding the mouse correctly? Are they using one finger on left button to click and drag-and-drop? Is their thumb on left side? Is mouse wheel free? Is their palm on bottom part of mouse?

_____Close down without saving. Go to installed keyboard software or online website for age-appropriate typing practice.

_____As you teach, remember to use correct vocabulary. Find opportunities during class to incorporate vocab highlighted for this lesson into teaching. Check this line item if you did that today!

_____Continually throughout class, check for understanding. Expect students to solve problems and make decisions.

_____Remind students to transfer this knowledge to classroom or home.

_____Tuck chairs under desk, headphones over tower; leave station as you found it.

Trouble-shooting:

- *Students can't get the door or window right? Left click and drag over and down, and drop. Guide their hands on the mouse to enable them to accomplish this.*
- *Sides of house aren't even (see inset)? Use boards to even them up (see inset at end of lesson).*
- *Trees came out purple? They match the color palette. Change the color selection to change their hue.*
- *Student can't finish? It doesn't matter to the goals we focus on with this project. If they're working on tools, toolbars, mouse skills, they're succeeding!*
- *Students finish early? Have them create a birthday card in their drawing program for someone using skills they know.*
- *Your drawing program doesn't include these tools? Adapt to what you have that will accomplish the Big Idea—sharing information with pictures.*
- *You have print book and need website? Pick grade level and search (Ctrl+F) name on http://ow.ly/j0WEA.*

Extension:

- *Add something in window. What would show through from street? (see inset in Lesson 23 for example).*
- *Add landscaping like trees and grass.*
- *Have students who display difficulty with mouse skills practice on these websites:*
-

  - *More Mouse Skills*
  - *Mousing around*
  - *Mouse basics—video*
  - *Mouse Click Skills*
  - *Mouse practice*

  - *Mouse drag, click*
  - *Mouse Song*
  - *Mouse Use Video*
  - *Mouse—Tidy the Classroom*
  - *Mouse—Wack a Gopher*

- *If this lesson doesn't work for your student group, use one from **How to Jumpstart the Inquiry-based Classroom.** It has 5 additional projects for Kindergarten (and all grades) aligned with the SL curriculum.*

More Information:
- *Lesson questions? Go to http://askatechteacher.com*
- *Kindergarten teaching wiki:*
  http://smaatechk-3.wikispaces.com/This+Week+in+Tech—Kindergarten
- *PDF: See appendix for bonus websites*
- *Follow keyboard lessons in K-8 Keyboard Curriculum (http://ow.ly/j6GH8)*

If you don't get through everything, check completed items so you know what to get back to when you have time on later lessons. I find as I focus on the central idea of a lesson, clarifying questions sometimes take more time than I'd expect. I'm fine with that. There'll be lessons later that move faster than I planned.

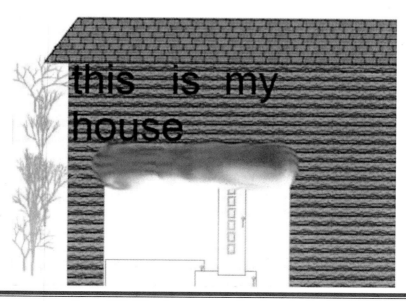

Lesson #23—Open House: My House II

Vocabulary	Problem solving	Big Idea
Architecture	My program disappeared (check taskbar at bottom of screen)	Details strengthen communication
Building tools	I can't find icon on desktop (try Start button)	
Delete key		
Edit	I can't delete a detail in my drawing (paint over it)	
Icon		
Lessons	My volume doesn't work (check volume control on systray)	
Start button		
Wacky tool		

Time Required	NETS-S Standards	CCSS
45 minutes	1b, 6b	CCSS.ELA-Literacy.W.K.5

Essential Question

How can I help others understand my drawings and writing?

Overview

Materials

Internet, drawing program, printer, keyboarding program, Kerpoof (if doing extension)

Teacher Preparation

- Based on last week's drafts, understand what details help students communicate their ideas better
- Have link to Kerpoof on class start page if doing extension
- Is class shorter than 45 minutes? Highlight items most important to your integration with core classroom studies and leave the rest for 'later'.

Steps

_____This is the second time students will create this drawing. They use textures available under paint brush. They will export this week.

_____Remind students about Open House slideshow project, where they publish their work and share it with friends and family.

_____Open KidPix (or whatever drawing program you use at your school) using desktop icon or Start button icon (what's the difference?).

_____Use paint brush construction tools like bricks, boards, windows, doors, roof, to build house. Do as independently as possible. Remind students that they know how to do it.

_____Drag and drop letters from animation tool for 'My House' onto screen.

_____When student thinks they are done, evaluate whether it has the details required to uniquely represent their 'house'.

_____Done evaluating? Ask a neighbor for assistance. What does this second person see when they look at classmate's drawing? What do they think would make it clearer (see inset—neighbor suggested the addition of rainbow)? Have student revise details based on input.

_____Export—with assistance if needed.

_____Finished? Go to keyboarding software or online site. Observe students for correct posture, hand position, fingers curved over home row.

_____As you teach, incorporate lesson vocabulary. Check this line if you did that today!

_____Continually throughout class, check for understanding. Expect students to solve problems and make decisions that follow class rules.

_____Remind students to transfer knowledge to classroom or home.

_____Close to desktop. Tuck chairs under desk, headphones over tower; leave station as you found it.

Assessment Strategies
- *Anecdotal*
- *Worked well in a group*
- *Used knowledge from prior lessons*
- *Understood each student work is unique*
- *Digital tools conveyed important information*
- *Completed project*

Trouble-shooting:
- *Student doesn't think drawing looks good/real? Remind him/her that each drawing is unique. It shouldn't look like any other student's.*
- *Drawing program won't allow saving? Take a screen shot and save that (using Jing, Snippet, or similar).*
- *You have print book and need website? Pick grade level and search (Alt+F) name on https://askatechteacher.wordpress.com/great-websites-for-kids/.*

Extension:
- *Use landscape tools if there's time (see inset).*
- *Use this second week as a formative assessment. What do students remember of skills practiced last week?*
- *Use online program (i.e., Kerpoof) to explore student story options.*
- *If this lesson doesn't work for your students, use one from **How to Jumpstart the Inquiry-based Classroom.** It has 5 projects aligned with the SL curriculum.*

More Information:
- *Lesson questions? Go to http://askatechteacher.com*
- *Kindergarten teaching wiki: http://smaatechk-3.wikispaces.com/This+Week+in+Tech—Kindergarten*
- *PDF: See appendix for bonus websites*
- *Follow keyboard lessons in K-8 Keyboard Curriculum (http://ow.ly/j6GH8)*
- *Full digital citizenship curriculum for kindergarten available here (http://www.structuredlearning.net/book/k-8-digital-citizenship-curriculum/)*

If you don't get through everything, check completed items so you know what to get back to when you have time on later lessons. I find as I focus on the central idea of a lesson, clarifying questions sometimes take more time than I'd expect. I'm fine with that. There'll be lessons later that move faster than I planned.

Lesson #24—Stamps and More

Vocabulary	Problem solving	Big Idea
▪ Curved hands ▪ Delete key ▪ Desktop icon ▪ Edit ▪ Export ▪ Font size ▪ Home row ▪ Parallel ▪ Stamps ▪ Start button ▪ Taskbar ▪ Text tool ▪ Vehicles	▪ Program disappeared (check taskbar) ▪ My sound doesn't work (do you have the right headphones on) ▪ I don't like the fill I picked (click Oops Guy right away. He only undoes one step) ▪ My fill went in the wrong places (snug lines to edges) ▪ I can't get it to look right (use your imagination) ▪ I can't find stamps (can you find the first letter of the category—i.e., 'v' for 'vehicles'?)	*Images can more fully share details of an experience*
Time Required *45 minutes*	**NETS-S Standards** *1a, 1b, 6d*	**CCSS** *CCSS.ELA-Literacy.W.K.8*

Essential Question
How do images help with understanding?

Overview

Materials

Internet, drawing program, keyboarding program

Teacher Preparation
- Place websites on internet start page that tie in with classroom inquiry
- Make sure student network folders are accessible
- Is class shorter than 45 minutes? Highlight items most important to your integration with core classroom studies and leave the rest for 'later'.

Steps

_____This is the last drawing for Open House project, to share the range of technology skills learned in kindergarten. This one uses a variety including fills, stamps and pencil tool. Because of the practice students have had with fills, plan to finish this in one day.

_____Demonstrate how to draw the hometown street. Remind them a street has two sides so draw two lines by each other, somewhat parallel (what's parallel?) Show what happens if they don't snug street lines to side of canvas (fill spills over between sections). Remind them where the realistic fills are (from Lesson 20). Take suggestions on how to fill the street, the ground, and the sky.

_____Discuss what students find in their neighborhood. Pets? Toys? Cars? Discuss this as a group. Encourage students to think about what they have seen on the streets, the yards, where they go with family. Find these stamps to add to their drawing.

_____Have students open KidPix (or drawing program used at your school. Be sure it has options for realistic fills and stamps) with desktop icon or Start button icon. Work as independently as possible.

_____Using pencil tool, select thick and a dark color. Draw street. Be sure ends are flush with side of screen. Use bucket fill—3rd bucket—to fill sky, road, ground. Explore options. Oops your choice if it doesn't work out.

_____Place appropriate stamps and stickers where they belong in neighborhood. Use dots (large-larger-largest) on lower toolbar to change stamp size.

_____As students work, help them recall what objects they would find around their home. Or experiences—like going to the beach would require a car to get there and a beach umbrella.

_____Drag and drop animated letters for 'My Town' (or 'My Neighborhood') onto screen.

_____When student thinks they are done, have them ask a neighbor for assistance. What does this second person see when they look at their classmate's drawing? What do they think would make it clearer (see inset—neighbor suggested addition of sun because it went along with beach umbrella)? Have student revise details based on input.

_____Export. Don't print—this is a surprise for parents.

_____Done? Practice keyboarding on installed software or online site. Use correct posture.

_____As you teach, incorporate lesson vocabulary. Check this line if you did that today!

_____Continually throughout class, check for understanding. Expect students to solve problems as they maneuver through the lesson and make decisions that follow class rules.

_____Close to desktop.

_____Remind students to transfer knowledge to classroom or home.

_____Tuck chairs under desk, headphones over tower; leave station as you found it.

Assessment Strategies

- *Anecdotal*
- *Worked well in groups*
- *Completed project*
- *Revised project based on input*
- *Transferred knowledge from prior lessons*
- *Joined class conversation*

Trouble-shooting:

- *Drawing program won't allow saving? Take a screen shot and save that (using Jing, Snippet, or similar).*
- *Drawing program doesn't have fills? See sample at end of lesson.*
- *You have print book and need website? Pick grade level and search (Alt+F) name on https://askatechteacher.wordpress.com/great-websites-for-kids/.*
- *Sometimes you need more than one week for a lesson. No worries. There are 32 lessons in text, 35ish in school year. Feel free to stretch a lesson a week or more.*

Extension:

- *Finished typing practice? Have websites on class start page that tie in with inquiry.*
- *If this lesson doesn't work for your student group, use one from* **How to Jumpstart the Inquiry-based Classroom.** *It has 5 additional projects for Kindergarten (and all grades) aligned with the SL curriculum.*

More Information:
- *Lesson questions? Go to http://askatechteacher.com*
- *Kindergarten teaching wiki:*
  http://smaatechk-3.wikispaces.com/This+Week+in+Tech—Kindergarten
- *PDF: See appendix for bonus websites*
- *Follow keyboard lessons in K-8 Keyboard Curriculum (http://ow.ly/j6GH8)*

If you don't get through everything, check completed items so you know what to get back to when you have time on later lessons. I find as I focus on the central idea of a lesson, clarifying questions sometimes take more time than I'd expect. I'm fine with that. There'll be lessons later that move faster than I planned.

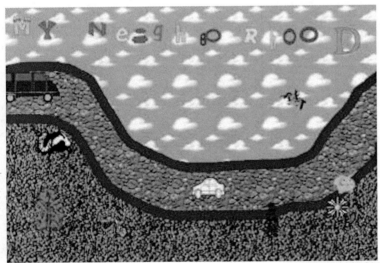

Lesson #25—Greeting Cards I

Vocabulary	Problem solving	Big Idea
Alphabet Animation tool Background Greeting Greeting card Toolbar Tools	How do I print? (Ctrl+P or file-print) I can't find the file I saved (use Windows 'search' function) I can't find file from last week (where did you save it? Your network folder?) The stamp is too big (Use the small-medium-large dot to change size)	Greeting cards are a great way to learn and reinforce tech skills required for lots of activities
Time Required 45 minutes	**NETS-S Standards** 1b, 2b	**CCSS** CCSS.ELA-Literacy.L.K.2

Essential Question
How can basic tech skills be fun?

Overview

Materials

Internet, drawing program, printer

Teacher Preparation

- Know what grammar conventions kindergarteners have learned so you can reinforce
- Is class shorter than 45 minutes? Highlight items most important to your integration with core classroom studies and leave the rest for 'later'.

Steps

_____Today, students will use tech skills to create an Easter card. Throughout the year, offer opportunities like this for students to reinforce learned skills by creating cards geared toward whichever holiday is occurring. They will be excited and work hard to remember how to use the tools so they can create a gift for their family/friends. Limit your assistance, rather challenge them to draw on their problem-solving skills.

_____Open a new canvas in the drawing program being used (samples are from KidPix).

_____Select a background that says 'Easter' to student. Have students try two options for decorating:

- *Use spray can to 'spray' bunnies, eggs, etc. around picture (remember using it for Valentine card?). See first inset. Don't bury picture in spray can items—we want to see it*
- *Use background tool to add Easter/Spring background (see second inset)*

_____When drawing is completed, add greeting (what's a greeting?) and student name. Demonstrate command of grammar and usage conventions being studied in class, i.e.:

- *Capitalize first word in a sentence and pronouns*
- *Recognize and name end punctuation*
- *Spell simple words phonetically, drawing on knowledge of sound-letter relationships*

_____As you teach, incorporate lesson vocabulary. Check this line if you did that!

_____Continually throughout class, check for understanding. Expect students to solve problems as they maneuver through lesson and make decisions following class rules.

_____Remind students to transfer knowledge to classroom or home.

_____ Print (*Ctrl+P if possible*). Close to desktop. Tuck chairs under desk, headphones over tower; leave station as you found it.

Trouble-shooting:
- *Too early for Easter? Create birthday cards for specific students or generic ones that can be passed out when the time comes. Or, swap this lesson with #26 and/or #27.*
- *Drawing program won't allow saving? Take a screen shot and save. (using Jing, Snippet, or similar).*
- *You have print book and need link? Pick grade level; search (Alt+F) name from https://askatechteacher.wordpress.com/great-websites-for-kids/.*
- *Sometimes you need more than one week for a lesson. No worries. There are 32 lessons in text, 35ish in school year. Feel free to stretch a lesson a week or more.*

Extension:
- *This—and all greeting card projects—can be used as formative assessments of student technology skills.*
- *If this lesson doesn't work for your student group, use one from* **How to Jumpstart the Inquiry-based Classroom.** *It has 5 additional projects for Kindergarten (and all grades) aligned with the SL curriculum.*

More Information:
- *Lesson questions? Go to http://askatechteacher.com*
- *Kindergarten teaching wiki: http://smaatechk-3.wikispaces.com/This+Week+in+Tech—Kindergarten*
- *PDF: See appendix for bonus websites*
- *Follow keyboard lessons in K-8 Keyboard Curriculum (http://ow.ly/j6GH8)*

If you don't get through everything, check completed items so you know what to get back to when you have time on later lessons. I find as I focus on the central idea of a lesson, clarifying questions sometimes take more time than I'd expect. I'm fine with that. There'll be lessons later that move faster than I planned.

Lesson #26—Intro to IPads

Vocabulary	Problem solving	Big Idea
• app • Apple • battery • boot-up • charger • dock • finger tap • Gorilla Glass • home button • iBook • iPads • jack • microphone • powering off • recharger • search • swipe • tablet	• How do I capitalize a word? (use shift key) • How do I add a period to end of a sentence (double tab space bar) • How do I get back to the home screen (push Home button) • I can't find an app I need (use Search) • I can't hear my video (plug headphones in) • How do I draw (with your finger) • Can't plug iPad into recharger (help students do this) • Class iPads are too noisy (plug headphones in) • How do I turn iPad off (close cover)	*Technology is more than computers in the class and/or lab*
Time Required *45 minutes*	**NETS-S Standards** *4c, 6d*	**CCSS** *Anchor Standards*

Essential Question
Can technology feel like part of life rather than an intimidating machine?

Overview

Materials

Wifi, iPads

Teacher Preparation

- Have required apps on class iPads
- Talk to classroom teacher to determine if there are any topics/apps they would like you to review with students
- Is class shorter than 45 minutes? Highlight items most important to your integration with core classroom studies and leave the rest for 'later'

Steps

_____What is an iPad? It's a brand name—not a product—for a tablet computer designed, developed and marketed by Apple and used primarily for audio-visual media such as books, games, periodicals, movies, music, and web content. It has a keyboard, but most people maneuver with finger taps and swipes.

_____It does less than other computers, but what it does is spectacular. Such as it's instantly on—no booting up. If you use your computer boot-up to take a break, that's over. It's big enough to watch videos, read a book. It isn't a phone, but can make phone calls through <u>Skype</u>. It isn't a camera, but takes great pictures.

_____Every new tech appliance needs a killer app. For iPads, it's running apps. Thousands— tens of thousands—of them, each with a particular corner on creativity and ingenuity.

_____Before handing iPads to students, make sure you understand what your school

expects of iPad use. Is it curriculum support or to change the way teaching is delivered? Are they to enhance pedagogy? And how will you assess success of iPad program? Know expectations so there are no surprises in the end.

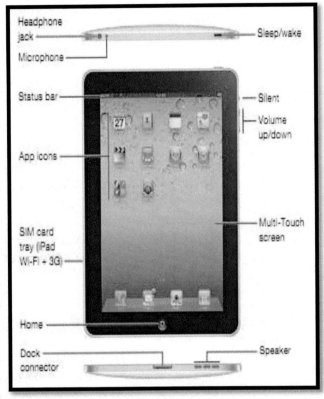

_____Start with an introduction, iPad in-hand (in groups if you like). Take a tour showing the screen (with apps, task bar at the bottom, search function revealed with right swipe), home button, recharger (make it student responsibility to put it back into iPad cart plugged into charger), front and back camera, microphone, jack for headphones—critical with 20 students in a room all using iPads, on/off, volume, dock.

_____Many students are familiar with iPads so ask about favorite uses. Remind students of class rules for group discussion:

- *listen to others speak*
- *take turns speaking*
- *wait to be called on before beginning*

_____As they share, demonstrate.

_____Brainstorm for best practices in using iPads in class, proper care, things students can do, but shouldn't at school. For example, don't drop or toss them.

_____Show students how to check battery. With a battery life approaching nine hours, that probably won't be an issue, but it's a good step to get used to.

_____Create a Scavenger Hunt of apps and functions you consider important to students. Let them work in pairs as they hunt. Be sure to include reading an ebook, taking a picture of a friend,

Assessment Strategies
- *Anecdotal*
- *Followed directions*
- *Displayed sense of engagement, risk-taking*
- *Worked well in groups*

taking a picture of themselves, watching a video. This is a self-paced activity, completely inquiry-driven. Be available for clarifying questions.

_____Let students explore apps. Roll into a discussion of volume controls, headphones. Here's a list   (http://askatechteacher.wordpress.com/great-apps/) used in many schools.

_____Establish a procedure for 'shutting down' iPads—similar to how students take care of computer station. Include cleaning screen, powering off, plugging into cart.

_____Remind students to transfer knowledge to classroom or home.

Trouble-shooting:

- *Students can't find app because there are so many? Teach them to use 'Search'.*
- *Watching a video and it's too loud with all the classroom iPads playing? Have students plug headphones in.*
- *How do you control students who use the iPad while you're teaching another subject? Have them close the cover.*
- *If this lesson doesn't work for your student group, use one from **How to Jumpstart the Inquiry-based Classroom.** It has 5 additional projects for Kindergarten (and all grades) aligned with the SL curriculum.*
- *You have print book and need website? Pick grade level and search (Alt+F) name on https://askatechteacher.wordpress.com/great-websites-for-kids/.*
- *Sometimes you need more than one week for a lesson. No worries. There are 32 lessons in text, 35ish in school year. Feel free to stretch a lesson a week or more.*

Extension:

- *As students suggest favorite activities, list them on SmartScreen as a 'to do' list.*
- *Have pdfs (in iBooks or other reader) for students to read.*

More Information:

- *Lesson questions? Go to http://askatechteacher.com*
- *Kindergarten teaching wiki: http://smaatechk-3.wikispaces.com/This+Week+in+Tech—Kindergarten*
- *PDF: See appendix for bonus websites*
- *Follow keyboard lessons in K-8 Keyboard Curriculum (http://ow.ly/j6GH8)*
- *Full digital citizenship curriculum for kindergarten available here (http://www.structuredlearning.net/book/k-8-digital-citizenship-curriculum/)*

If you don't get through everything, check completed items so you know what to get back to when you have time on later lessons. I find as I focus on the central idea of a lesson, clarifying questions sometimes take more time than I'd expect. I'm fine with that. There'll be lessons later that move faster than I planned.

"Error, no keyboard — press F1 to continue."

Lesson #27—Explore the Internet

Vocabulary	Problem solving	Big Idea
▪ 'Hand' ▪ Address ▪ Ads ▪ Back button ▪ Decode ▪ Digital citizen ▪ Digital neighborhood ▪ Internet ▪ Internet start page ▪ Links ▪ Search bar ▪ Start page ▪ Tabbed browsing	▪ Program disappeared (check taskbar) ▪ How do I use a website link (find the hand, click) ▪ I don't like where I am (use class start page tab to return to list) ▪ I don't like where I am in the website (use back arrow) ▪ I won a prize! (Discuss ads) ▪ I don't understand a word (use class strategies for decoding meaning)	*Stories have characters, settings, and major events that make them exciting to read*
Time Required *45 minutes*	**NETS-S Standards** *3c, 4c*	**CCSS** *CCSS.ELA-Literacy.RL.K.3*

Essential Question
How can I identify the characters, settings, and major events in a story?

Overview

Materials

Internet, reading websites, My Online Neighborhood link, keyboarding programs

Teacher Preparation
- Have link on internet start page for digital neighborhood and reading websites to be visited today
- Is class shorter than 45 minutes? Highlight items most important to your integration with core classroom studies and leave the rest for 'later'.

Steps

_____Practice keyboarding with installed software or online program. Use correct posture, hand position. Observe student habits and guide them.

_____Done? Students will read a story on the internet. But first, circle back on discussions about internet safety from Lessons 12 and 13. What do students remember about:

- *Using the internet*
- *Digital neighborhood*
- *Safety online*

_____Open internet to class internet start page. Ask students where the digital neighborhood is on this page? What should they avoid? Why?

_____Discuss the poster at the end of this lesson. How is the 'digital neighborhood' like their physical neighborhood?

_____Watch My Online Neighborhood (Google for address) as a group and discuss. What were the three rules the boy mentioned? How is this same/different from being a citizen of the student's home town? Where is this 'digital town'?

_____Click on one of the reading sites available for today's class. Show students how to correctly use the website:

- *Don't click on other websites (how can they identify those?)*
- *Don't click ads (what is an ad?)*
- *Stay in the 'digital neighborhood'*

_____Point out address bar at top of webpage, back arrow, home key. If there are ads, point them out so students know to avoid them.

_____Explore. Notice when cursor becomes a hand, that's a new place to visit.

_____Demo several websites and show students how to find stories at their reading level. If they pick one that doesn't work, use browser tab to return to start page.

_____Remind them as they read to think about:

- *Key details*
- *Characters*
- *Setting*
- *Major events*

_____Read one (short) story together and discuss the above bullet items as a group before students explore independently. Provide strategies for identifying these in a story. Answer clarifying questions.

_____Don't be afraid to try links. Students can't break anything—have fun.

_____As you teach, incorporate lesson vocabulary. Check this line if you did that today!

_____Continually throughout class, check for understanding. Expect students to solve problems and make decisions that follow class rules.

_____Remind students to transfer knowledge to classroom or home.

_____Tuck chairs under desk, headphones over tower; leave station as you found it.

Trouble-shooting:

- *If students have difficulty doing what you are teaching, ask why. And listen. You may be surprised by the answer.*
- *If this takes too long or frustrates some students, do it in groups.*
- *Some students just don't want to read? Let them practice keyboarding after about 20-25 minutes of reading.*

- *You have print book and need website? Pick grade level and search (Alt+F) name on https://askatechteacher.wordpress.com/great-websites-for-kids/.*
- *Sometimes you need more than one week for a lesson. No worries. There are 32 lessons in the text, 35ish in the school year. Feel free to stretch a lesson a week or more.*

Extension:
- *Ask students to tell you when they find a word they don't understand. Help them decode its meaning.*
- *Have students discuss characters, setting, plot of the story they read with classmates.*
- *If this lesson doesn't work for your student group, use one from **How to Jumpstart the Inquiry-based Classroom.** It has 5 additional projects for Kindergarten (and all grades) aligned with the SL curriculum.*
- *Some great kindergarten reading sites (Google for addresses):*

  - *Dr Seuss Seussville*
  - *Kinder Stories*
  - *Magic Keys—stories for youngers*
  - *Make a story (simple)*
  - *Mighty book storybooks*
  - *PBS Stories—Between the Lions*
  - *Starfall*

More Information:
- *Lesson questions? Go to http://askatechteacher.com*
- *Kindergarten teaching wiki: http://smaatechk-3.wikispaces.com/This+Week+in+Tech—Kindergarten*
- *PDF: See appendix for bonus websites*
- *Follow keyboard lessons in K-8 Keyboard Curriculum (http://ow.ly/j6GH8*
- *Full digital citizenship curriculum for kindergarten available here (http://www.structuredlearning.net/book/k-8-digital-citizenship-curriculum/)*

If you don't get through everything, check completed items so you know what to get back to when you have time on later lessons. I find as I focus on the central idea of a lesson, clarifying questions sometimes take more time than I'd expect. I'm fine with that. There'll be lessons later that move faster than I planned.

Compaq is considering changing the command "Press Any Key" to "Press Return Key" because of the many calls asking where the "Any" key is.

Don't talk to strangers. Look both ways before crossing the (virtual) street. Don't go places you don't know. Play fair. Pick carefully who you trust. Don't get distracted by bling. And sometimes, stop everything and take a nap.

Lesson #28—Internet Fairy Tales

lary	Problem solving	Big Idea
Character Compare/contrast Explorer Graphic organizer Icon Link Major events Setting	*My program froze (is there a dialogue box open?)* *My double-click doesn't work (push enter)* *My computer doesn't work (turn power on)* *My group won't let me talk (are you following rules class adopted for group discussion?)*	*Stories have characters, settings, and major events that are similar and different*
Time Required *45 minutes*	**NETS-S Standards** *2b, 3b*	**CCSS** *CCSS.ELA-Literacy.RL.K.9*

Essential Question
How can I compare and contrast setting and experiences of characters in stories?

Overview

Materials

Internet, fairy tale websites, images, graphic organizer, keyboarding program

Teacher Preparation

- Have generic images available for 'character', 'setting', 'plot' to use in graphic organizer
- Have a graphic organizer to compare/contrast characters, plot, setting
- Talk with classroom teacher so you tie into their conversations
- If you can get parent helpers, this is a good lesson to use them
- Is class shorter than 45 minutes? Highlight the items most important to your integration with core classroom studies and leave the rest for 'later'.

Steps

_____Practice keyboarding with installed software or online program. Use correct posture, hand position. Observe student habits and guide them.

_____Done? Students will read a story on the internet and explore details together, but first, circle back on discussions about internet safety from last week. What do students remember about:

- *Using the internet*
- *Digital neighborhood*
- *Safety online*

_____Open internet to <u>class home page</u> Have 3-4 fairy tales that collaborate with classroom discussion on this topic. Divide class into groups (rows or tables) and assign each group a fairy tale to read. Give them 5-10 minutes to read to themselves. Ask them to pay attention to characters, setting, major events.

_____When done, as a small group, take 5-10 minutes to discuss story parts—characters, setting, major events—with each other.

_____While they share, open three graphic organizers on SmartScreen (or one for each group). The inset is from Word, but you can use one from any number of free online sources, i.e.:

- *Graphic organizers*
- *Graphic organizers II*
- *Graphic Organizers III*

- *Graphic organizers—all topics*
- *Graphic organizers—Enchanted Learning*
- *Graphic Organizers—for reading*

_____Add pictures of three parts and title of each story being read.

_____When done, one at a time, groups share their thoughts on three elements of their story. As they share, add them to graphic organizer for class to see.

_____When all groups are done, discuss as a class what is alike and different about elements. Were characters similar? How about major events? Add lines that connect the pieces that are alike.

_____As you teach, incorporate lesson vocabulary. Check this line if you did that today!

_____Continually throughout class, check for understanding. Expect students to solve problems as they maneuver through the lesson and make decisions that follow class rules.

_____Remind students to transfer knowledge to classroom or home.

_____Tuck chairs under desk, headphones over tower; leave station as you found it.

Assessment Strategies
- *Anecdotal observation of keyboarding*
- *Participated in class conversations*
- *Identified key parts of stories*

Trouble-shooting:
- *You have print book and need website? Pick grade level and search (Alt+F) name on https://askatechteacher.wordpress.com/great-websites-for-kids/.*
- *Sometimes you need more than one week for a lesson. No worries. There are 32 lessons in text, 35ish in school year. Feel free to stretch a lesson a week or more.*

Extension:
- *Have groups read story aloud to each other rather than to themselves.*
- *Read stories on iPads if available. Remind students of Lesson 26 best practices. Let students curl into a comfortable reading setting if available.*
- *Extra time? Practice keyboarding on installed software or online program.*

- Anytime you can inject tech into the class, do it! Students love seeing gadgets in action. For example—take a video of students working at their computers and upload to class website/blog/wiki.
- If this lesson doesn't work for your student group, use one from **How to Jumpstart the Inquiry-based Classroom.** It has 5 additional projects for Kindergarten (and all grades) aligned with the SL curriculum.

More Information:

- Lesson questions? Go to http://askatechteacher.com
- Kindergarten teaching wiki: http://smaatechk-3.wikispaces.com/This+Week+in+Tech—Kindergarten
- PDF: See appendix for bonus websites
- Follow keyboard lessons in K-8 Keyboard Curriculum (http://ow.ly/j6GH8)
- Full digital citizenship curriculum for kindergarten available here (http://www.structuredlearning.net/book/k-8-digital-citizenship-curriculum/)

If you don't get through everything, check completed items so you know what to get back to when you have time on later lessons. I find as I focus on the central idea of a lesson, clarifying questions sometimes take more time than I'd expect. I'm fine with that. There'll be lessons later that move faster than I planned.

Login: yes
Password: I don't have one
password is incorrect

Login: yes
Password: incorrect
password is incorrect

Lesson #29—Windows Slideshows

Vocabulary	Problem solving	Big Idea
Class start page Clip-art Clock Desktop Digital tools Drill down Graphics Log-on Mac Operating system PC Slideshow Taskbar Wallpaper Windows	Program disappeared? (check taskbar) Where's my network folder (under 'computer') I right clicked and nothing happened (try 'other' right click) Someone changed my wallpaper (yes, that happens) I can't get out of slideshow (push escape) What's the difference between 'software' and 'internet'? (i.e., 'Windows' and class internet start page)	*I can use technology to publish the projects I completed this year and share them with everyone*
Time Required *45 minutes*	**NETS-S Standards** *2b, 6a*	**CCSS** *CCSS.ELA-Literacy.W.K.6*

Essential Question
How can I use a variety of digital tools to share my creativity with others?

Overview

Materials

Internet, Windows, collection of student projects, keyboarding program

Teacher Preparation

- Have all student projects collected in their network folder
- Is class shorter than 45 minutes? Highlight items most important to your integration with core classroom studies and leave the

Steps

_____Warm up with keyboarding on installed software or online programs. Remind students of correct posture, hand position.

_____Discuss types of computers (PC and Mac). Discuss operating system that makes each unique. Why do people love Macs/PCs better than the alternative? Discuss what students use at home and how it compares to school systems.

_____What does 'windows' mean? Where are these windows?

_____Review Windows (or Macs if you have a Mac school)—basic operating system for PC computers (see inset).

- *Taskbar—shows open programs (tasks)*
- *Clock—hover to see date*

- *Start button—click for more programs*
- *Wallpaper—easily changed, especially by older students who know how*

_____Give students a few moments to explore Windows parts.

_____Now show students how to access their projects from computer Start button and run a slideshow of pictures using Windows.

_____Demo first and then have students follow along:

- *Go to Start button, 'Computer'. Drill down to student folder*
- *Double-click jpg file*
- *Click slideshow button at bottom center*

_____Slideshow will play until students pushes escape to end it.

_____Have them try this a second time without help. Do with a neighbor. Remind them of class rules for talking as a group. Discuss pictures with each other. Explain which digital tools were used to create the drawing. Each may ask questions of the other's slideshow. Answer with detail that addresses questions. This will prepare students for questions parents are likely to ask.

_____Have students get into their slideshow every week until Open House.

_____Done? Visit websites on start page student would like to take parents to.

_____Close down to desktop.

_____As you teach, incorporate lesson vocab. Check this line if you did that!

_____Continually throughout class, check for understanding. Expect students to solve problems as they maneuver through the lesson and make decisions that follow class rules.

_____Remind students to transfer knowledge to classroom or home.

_____Tuck chairs under desk, headphones over tower; leave station as you found it.

Trouble-shooting:
- *You have print book and need website? Pick grade level and search (Alt+F) name on https://askatechteacher.wordpress.com/great-websites-for-kids/.*
- *Sometimes you need more than one week for a lesson. No worries. There are 32 lessons in text, 35ish in the school year. Feel free to stretch a lesson a week or more.*

Extension:
- *Show students how to right click on an image and change wallpaper. Have them change wallpaper to one of their drawings. Everyone won't get this. That's fine.*

- If this lesson doesn't work for your student group, use one from **How to Jumpstart the Inquiry-based Classroom.** It has 5 additional projects for Kindergarten (and all grades) aligned with the SL curriculum.

More Information:
- Lesson questions? Go to http://askatechteacher.com
- Kindergarten teaching wiki:
  http://smaatechk-3.wikispaces.com/This+Week+in+Tech—Kindergarten
- PDF: See appendix for bonus websites
- Follow keyboard lessons in K-8 Keyboard Curriculum (http://ow.ly/j6GH8)

If you don't get through everything, check completed items so you know what to get back to when you have time on later lessons. I find as I focus on the central idea of a lesson, clarifying questions sometimes take more time than I'd expect. I'm fine with that. There'll be lessons later that move faster than I planned.

"Teachers are expected to reach unattainable goals with inadequate tools. The miracle is that at times they accomplish this impossible task."

—Haim G. Ginott

Lesson #30—Greeting Cards II

Vocabulary	Problem solving	Big Idea
Backspace Click Delete Edit Format Grammar Greeting Greeting card Network Skills Text tool	*Computer doesn't work (is power on?)* *Monitor doesn't work (is power on?)* *Volume doesn't work (check control on systray)* *Capital doesn't work (is caps lock on?)* *I can't find drawing program (where was it last time?)* *What's the difference between backspace and delete?* *What's the difference between edit and format?*	*Greeting cards are a great way to learn and reinforce tech skills required for lots of activities*
Time Required *45 minutes*	**NETS-S Standards** *1b, 2c*	**CCSS** *CCSS.ELA-Literacy.L.K.2*

Essential Question
How—and when—can basic tech skills be fun to learn?

Overview

Materials

Internet, drawing program, printer, student class pictures (if following extension), internet start page

Teacher Preparation

- Have student pictures available on network if using extension
- Know what grammar conventions are expected of students by this point in year
- Is class shorter than 45 minutes? Highlight items most important to your integration with core classroom studies and leave the rest for 'later'.

Steps

_____Start class by practicing slideshow of student drawings in Windows slideshow program. Have students practice, then do it for their neighbor while other students are finishing.

_____Create a greeting card using skills learned throughout the year. This can be done independently, with you available to clarify, but not problem solve (unless necessary).

_____Ask students to think back on skills learned and use them to create a Mother's Day/Memorial Day card.

Be risk takers—be problem-solvers if they get stuck. Guide students if necessary, but resist the urge to tell. They know. They just have to think about it. If card doesn't come out quite like students wanted, it doesn't matter. It's unique.

_____Open drawing program. We use KidPix. Use paint brush, 5 brushes and 5 colors.

_____Add a frame. Draw student picture inside frame.

_____Have students pause in their work (I have them turn off their monitors so they aren't distracted) while you bring a sample up on SmartScreen. Add greeting with misspelled words and poor grammar conventions. Ask students for help fixing it.

_____Students finish cards by adding greeting with text tool and their name with 'dog alphabet'. Watch grammar and spelling. Edit if required with backspace and delete.

_____Students print by themselves and export.

_____Done? Go to websites on internet start page and practice those that students wish to take their parents to at Open House.

_____As you teach, incorporate lesson vocabulary. Check this line if you did that today!

_____Continually throughout class, check for understanding. Expect students to solve problems as they maneuver through the lesson and make decisions that follow class rules.

_____Remind students to transfer knowledge to classroom or home.

_____Tuck chairs under desk, headphones over tower; leave station as you found it.

Assessment Strategies
- *Anecdotal*
- *Understood expected grammar conventions*
- *Completed project*
- *Transferred knowledge from prior lessons*

Trouble-shooting:
- *Student can't find drawing program? Teach how to use start button 'search'. They will want this skill for Open House.*
- *You have print book and need website? Pick grade level and search (Alt+F) name on https://askatechteacher.wordpress.com/great-websites-for-kids/.*
- *Sometimes you need more than one week for a lesson. No worries. There are 32 lessons in text, 35ish in school year. Feel free to stretch a lesson a week or more.*

Extension:
- *Add student picture inside of frame instead of drawing it.*
- *This—and all greeting card projects—can be used as formative assessments of student technology skills.*
- *If this lesson doesn't work for your student group, use one from **How to Jumpstart the Inquiry-based Classroom.** It has 5 additional projects for Kindergarten (and all grades) aligned with the SL curriculum.*

More Information:
- *Lesson questions? Go to http://askatechteacher.com*
- *Kindergarten teaching wiki: http://smaatechk-3.wikispaces.com/This+Week+in+Tech—Kindergarten*

- PDF: See appendix for bonus websites
- Follow keyboard lessons in _K-8 Keyboard Curriculum_ (_http://ow.ly/j6GH8_)

If you don't get through everything, check completed items so you know what to get back to when you have time on later lessons. I find as I focus on the central idea of a lesson, clarifying questions sometimes take more time than I'd expect. I'm fine with that. There'll be lessons later that move faster than I planned.

YOU KNOW YOU'RE LIVING IN THE 21ST CENTURY WHEN:

1. Your reason for not staying in touch with family is because they do not have e-mail addresses.
2. You have a list of 15 phone numbers to reach your family of three.
3. You call your son to let him know it's time to eat. He e-mails you back from his bedroom, "What's for dinner?"
4. Your daughter sells Girl Scout Cookies via her web site.
5. You chat several times a day with a stranger from South Africa, but you haven't spoken with your next door neighbor yet this year.
6. Leaving the house without your cell phone, which you didn't have the first 20 or 30 years of your life, is now a cause for panic and you turn around to go get it.
7. Using real money, instead of credit or debit, to make a purchase would be a hassle and takes planning.
8. You hear most of your jokes via e-mail instead of in person.
9. You get an extra phone line so you can get phone calls.
10. You disconnect from the Internet and get this awful feeling, as if you just pulled the plug on a loved one.
11. You get up in morning and go on-line before getting your coffee.
12. You wake up at 2 AM to go to the bathroom and check your E-mail on your way back to bed.
13. You're reading this.

Lesson #31—Shapes in My World

Vocabulary	Problem solving	Big Idea
🔲 *2D* 🔲 *3D* 🔲 *Cube* 🔲 *Pyramid*	🔲 *Screen froze (is dialogue box open?)* 🔲 *Capitals don't work (Check caps lock)*	**Shapes are the basis for many items found around us**
Time Required *45 minutes*	**NETS-S Standards** *3b, 6b*	**CCSS** *CCSS.Math.Content.K.G.A.1A*

Essential Question
Does the orientation or position of a shape change what it is?

Overview

Materials

Internet, drawing program, SmartScreen, printer, intra-school field trip

Teacher Preparation

- Have parent helpers for Shape Stroll
- Prepare as though for school field trip
- Know what shapes students have discussed this year and where they can be found around the campus
- Is class shorter than 45 minutes? Highlight the items most important to your integration with core classroom studies and leave the rest for 'later'.

Steps

_____Start class by practicing slideshow of student drawings in Windows. Students should be pretty good at it by now!

_____Students take a 'shape stroll' around school to discover shapes discussed in class.

_____Be sure to have extra helpers so students don't get separated.

_____Walk around school grounds and ask students to point out where they see squares, rectangles, circles, diamonds, cubes, pyramids and other shapes discussed in class. As you scribe for them, ask them to describe the relative positions of these objects using terms such as *above*, *below*, *beside*, *in front of*, *behind*, and *next to*.

_____Return to classroom and list shapes found on SmartScreen. Ask students to remind you where they saw them (front of building, beside athletic field, on top of tower, etc.). Jog their memories if necessary.

_____Have students draw one of the shapes and the surrounding item—building, play structure, window, etc.

_____Add their name to picture. Export and print.

_____As you teach, incorporate lesson vocabulary. Check this line if you did that today!

_____Continually throughout class, check for understanding. Expect students to solve problems as they maneuver through the lesson and make decisions that follow class rules.

_____Remind students to transfer knowledge to classroom or home.

_____Tuck chairs under desk, headphones over tower; leave station as you found it.

Trouble-shooting:

- *Students get distracted on Stroll? Train parents on how to keep students on task—gently—while they are exploring the school.*
- *You have print book and need website? Pick grade level and search (Alt+F) name on https://askatechteacher.wordpress.com/great-websites-for-kids/.*
- *Sometimes you need more than one week for a lesson. No worries. There are 32 lessons in the text, 35ish in the school year. Feel free to stretch a lesson a week or more.*

Extension:

- *Use iPad to list shapes found on campus during Stroll. Then, project iPad screen onto SmartScreen. Any time you can use technology in a 'cool' way—do it!*
- *Draw shapes of objects found on school grounds on SmartScreen, but change their orientation, position, size. Can students still identify what they see?*
- *Have drawing websites like Kerpoof available on class internet start page so students can draw more shapes.*
- *If this lesson doesn't work for your student group, use one from **How to Jumpstart the Inquiry-based Classroom.** It has 5 additional projects for Kindergarten (and all grades) aligned with the SL curriculum.*

More Information:

- *Lesson questions? Go to http://askatechteacher.com*
- *Kindergarten teaching wiki: http://smaatechk-3.wikispaces.com/This+Week+in+Tech—Kindergarten*
- *PDF: See appendix for bonus websites*
- *Follow keyboard lessons in K-8 Keyboard Curriculum (http://ow.ly/j6GH8)*

If you don't get through everything, check completed items so you know what to get back to when you have time on later lessons. I find as I focus on the central idea of a lesson, clarifying questions sometimes take more time than I'd expect. I'm fine with that. There'll be lessons later that move faster than I planned.

Lesson #32—Summative

Vocabulary	Problem solving	Big Idea
Tool *Brush* *Internet* *Icon* *Slideshow* *Image*	*Screen froze (Is a dialogue box open? Is program blinking on task bar?)* *My program disappeared (Check taskbar)* *Double-click doesn't work (Push enter)*	*Pictures require clarification and everyone doesn't understand what they see the same way. It's good to clarify details and answer questions.*
Time Required *45 minutes*	**NETS-S Standards** *3b, 6b*	**CCSS** *CCSS.ELA-Literacy.SL.K.6*

Essential Question
How can key questions from interested people help to clarify a message?

Overview

Materials

Internet, certificates, website links, drawing program

Teacher Preparation
- Have all certificates created for student kindergarten tech graduation
- Invite parents to watch how children know their skills
- Have slideshows ready to go

Steps

_____Students have a normal lesson with parents watching, everything shorter than usual so there is time to award certificates and watch slideshows.

_____Warm up with keyboarding on installed software or online program.

_____Let students draw anything they'd like in KidPix, to be printed for parents.

_____Students share slideshow as practiced. Describe their drawings, what they represent, and additional detail student feels is important. Answer parent questions to clarify images and key details.

_____Award certificates (see sample, end of text).

_____Done? Share any websites on start page with parents.

_____Tuck chairs under desk, headphones over tower; leave station as it was. Have a great summer!

Assessment Strategies
- *Anecdotal*

Trouble-shooting:
- *Student can't find folder? Be available to help where needed.*

Extension:
- *Show slideshows on SmartScreen.*

- *Have students narrate their slideshow while it plays in SmartScreen.*

More Information:
- *Lesson questions? Go to http://askatechteacher.com*
- *Kindergarten teaching wiki:*
  http://smaatechk-3.wikispaces.com/This+Week+in+Tech—Kindergarten
- *PDF: See appendix for bonus websites*

If you don't get through everything, check completed items so you know what to get back to when you have time on later lessons. I find as I focus on the central idea of a lesson, clarifying questions sometimes take more time than I'd expect. I'm fine with that. There'll be lessons later that move faster than I planned.

Compaq is considering changing the command "Press Any Key" to "Press Return Key" because of the many calls asking where the "Any" key is.

PS

If you teach technology, it's likely you're a geek. Even if you didn't start out that way–say, you used to be a first grade teacher and suddenly your Admin in their infinite wisdom, moved you to the tech lab—you became a geek. You morphed into the go-to person for tech problems, computer quirks, crashes and freezes.

Overnight, your colleagues assumed you received an upload of data that allowed 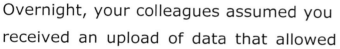 you to Know the answers to their every techie question. It didn't matter that yesterday, you were one of them. Now, you are on a pedestal, their necks craned upward as they ask you, *How do I get the SmartScreen to work?* or *We need the microphones working for a lesson I'm starting in three minutes. Can you please-please-please fix them?*

Celebrate your cheeky geekiness. Flaunt it for students and colleagues. Play Minecraft. That's you now–you are sharp, quick-thinking. You tingle when you see an iPad. You wear a flash drive like jewelry. The first thing you do when you get to school is check your email

It's OK. Here at Structured Learning and Ask a Tech Teacher, we understand. The readers understand. You're at home. To honor you, we've created these two posters (see next pages). They provide more ways to get your geek fully on as you go through your day.

10 steps To become A BETTER GEEK

1. Use **Tech**
2. Use **it** every day--save some trees
3. Use **it** when it seems difficult
4. Use **it** in class--and at home
5. Use **Tech** now--right now
6. Use **it** instead of something else
7. Teach a friend to use **it**
8. Teach a lot of friends to use **it**
9. Make **it** your first choice
10. Keep using **it**

15 ways

To GET YOUR GEEK ON

1. Be smart. Yeah, it feels good
2. That's my inner Geek speaking
3. Think. Exercise your brain.
4. Waves. Sigh.
5. Keep repeating, *People are my friends*. Like Siri.
6. Move away from the keyboard--Not.
7. Some people watch TV. I play with a Rubik's Cube
8. Be patient. I'm buffering.
9. There must be a shortkey for that
10. Life needs an Undo key
11. Leave me alone for 2 minutes and I'll go to sleep
12. Yes, I can fix your computer
13. Like a computer, I do what you tell me to
14. My RAM is full. Come back later.
15. Slow down. My processor isn't that fast

CONGRATULATIONS!

You have completed all requirements for Kindergarten Technology, including:

* Mouse skills
* Tools and toolbars
* Intro to Internet

* Intro do digital citizenship
* Intro to keyboarding
* Intro to Windows

_____
Signature

_____
Date

INTERNET SITES

These are bonus websites for PDF customers. Ctrl+click to access. If you have print version: Visit _Ask a Tech Teacher_ website for these links and updates (http://askatechteacher.com).

Please be aware: Links constantly change. Let us know if you find one that requires an update!

1. Aesop Fables
2. Aesop Fables—no ads
3. Alphabet Animals
4. Alphabet Doors
5. Animal Games
6. Animal Games II
7. Animal Homes II
8. Audio stories
9. Barnaby and Belinda Bear
10. Bembo's Zoo
11. Build a car
12. Build a car—abcya
13. Build a Neighborhood
14. Car puzzle
15. Clock games—many
16. Clocks
17. Clocks—set the time—BBC
18. Color US Symbols
19. Counting Money
20. Create Music
21. Dino collection
22. Dino Fossils then and now
23. Dino Games
24. Dino Games II
25. Dinosaurs
26. Dinosaurs II
27. Dinosaurs IV
28. Dinosaurs V
29. Dinosaurs VI
30. Dr. Seuss
31. Edugames at Pauly's Playhouse
32. Edugames—drag-and-drop puzzles
33. Endangered species collection
34. Fables—beautiful
35. Find a dog
36. Game Goo—wacky games that teach
37. Games to teach mouse skills, problem-solving
38. Games to teach problem-solving skills
39. Geogreeting—find letters around the world
40. Great Websites—can't get thru all of them
41. Groundhog Day
42. Holiday Elf Games
43. Holiday music
44. Holiday—Design Gingerbread House
45. Holiday—match game
46. Holiday—North Pole Academy
47. Holidays—various
48. Interactive sites
49. Kerpoof
50. Keyboarding—Hyper Spider Typing
51. Kindergarten Links—Science, etc.
52. KinderSite—lots of kindergarten websites
53. Learn to Read
54. Letters—find the letter
55. Letters—find the letter—caps and lower case
56. Letters—sort by sounds
57. Literacy sites
58. Magic Keys—stories for youngers
59. Make a Face
60. Make a Monster
61. Make a Scary Spud
62. Make a Story
63. Math for K
64. Math Games
65. Math/LA Videos by grade level
66. Mighty book storybooks
67. Mr. Picasso Head
68. Museum of Modern Art
69. Music—Quincy and the Magic Instruments
70. Ocean Currents—video from NASA
71. Ocean Safari
72. Ocean Tracks
73. PBS Stories—Between the Lions
74. Puzzle
75. Reading games
76. Shapes and colors
77. Sid the Scientist
78. Signed stories
79. Starfall
80. Stories—CircleTime—international
81. Stories—MeeGenius—read/to me
82. Stories—non-text
83. The Learning Planet
84. Time
85. Time clocks
86. Transportation alphabet
87. Transportation games
88. Transportation matching
89. Transportation Sequence Games
90. Transportation video—BrainPopJr
91. Turkey websites
92. Valentine Sudoku
93. Valentine mouse skills
94. Line up the hearts

95. Dress up the heart
96. Valentine unscramble
97. Valentine typing
98. Valentine puppy jigsaw
99. Valentine drag-and-drop
100. Valentine match
101. Valentine tic-tac-toe
102. Valentine projects from Winter Wonderland
103. Write in a heart
104. More heart writing
105. 'I love you' in languages Afrikaans to Zulu

106. Valentine's Day apps
107. Valentine Day games and stories
108. Valentine coloring book
109. Valentine Day poem generator
110. Valentine rebuses
111. Valentine rebus game
112. Virtual Farm
113. Virtual Zoo
114. Word games—k-2
115. Writing games
116. Ziggity Zoom Stories

Technology

1. Audio books—Ms. Noor—free
2. Bees and Honey
3. Clicky's Web(safe) World
4. Clicky's Web(safe) World II
5. Computer basics
6. Computer Basics II
7. Computer puzzle
8. Computer safety
9. Cyber-bullying video
10. Day in a digital citizen's life
11. Disney CyberNetiquette Comix
12. Drag and drop games—visual
13. Drag and drop puzzles
14. Drag and drop skills
15. Find the Technology
16. Garfield internet safety
17. Internet—what is it—video
18. Internet safety games
19. Internet Safety Site —Disney
20. Internet Smart Princess
21. Jigsaw puzzles
22. Jigzone—puzzles
23. Keyboard Climber
24. Keyboard Use Video

25. Listen/read—Free non-fic audio books
26. Monitor Use Video
27. More Mouse Skills
28. Mouse and tech basics—video
29. Mouse Click Skills—gorgeous
30. Mouse exercises—for olders too
31. Mouse practice
32. Mouse practice—drag, click
33. Mouse Song
34. Mouse Use Video
35. Mouse—Tidy the Classroom
36. Mouse—Wack a Gopher
37. Mousing around
38. My Online Neighborhood—video
39. NetSmartKids—read-to-you
40. Organize technology (drag and drop)
41. Parts of the computer
42. Parts of the computer—BrainPopJr
43. Princess who knew UYN—video
44. Surf Swell Island
45. Tech Training—basics
46. Tidy the classroom
47. Videos on Computer Basics K-6
48. Webville Outlaws—internet safety

For Teachers

1. Audio books—free—Project Gutenberg
2. Art on your Whiteboard
3. Blogs—Wordpress Classroom blogs
4. Brainstorming—Spicy Nodes
5. Coloring pages
6. Enchanted Learning
7. Google Safe Search Preferences
8. Google Sketch up projects

9. Internet Movie Database
10. PBS Learning Resources
11. Protopage Blog
12. Random Team Generator
13. Teaching Channel
14. Virtual tour—White House on GE
15. White Board—no sign in, no reg
16. YouTube for Education

SL Technology Books for your Classroom

Structured Learning K-8 Curriculum

Which book?	Price (print/digital/ Combo)	How Many?
Kindergarten-5th Tech Textbook (each)	$29.99/23.99/48.58 + p&h	
6th Grade Tech Textbook	$31.99/23.99/50.38 + p&h	
K-6 Combo (all 7 textbooks)	$190.74/151.14/341.87 + p&h	
35 More Projects for K-6 (aligned w cur)	$31.99/25.99/52.18 + p&h	
55 Tech Projects—Volume I or Volume II	$36.99/$24.99/$55.99 + p&h	
Volume I/II Combo	$66.99/$44.99/$111.97 + p&h	
K-8 Keyboard Curriculum	$29.95/23.99/48.55 + p&h	
K-8 Digital Citizenship Curriculum	$29.95/23.99/48.55 + p&h	
K-5 Common Core Lesson	$29.95/23.99/48.58 + p&h	
38 Web 2.0 Articles	$2.99 (digital only) + p&h	
16 Holiday Projects	$14.99 (digital only) + p&h	
19 Posters for the Tech Lab	$6.99 (digital only)	
18 More Posters for the Tech Lab	$12.99 (digital only)	
98 Tech Tips From Classroom	$9.99 (digital only) + p&h	
760+ Websites to Kick start Tech Ed	$14.99 (digital only) + p&h	
Tech Ed Scope and Sequences	$14.99 (digital only) + p&h	
New Teacher Survival Kit (K-5)	$338.21/284.28/563.51+ p&h	
New Teacher Survival Kit (K-6)	$370.20/308.27/613.90 + p&h	
New Teacher Survival Kit (6-8)	$282.83/252.87/408.78 + p&h	
Bundles of lesson plans	$7.99 and up	
Mentoring (1 hr. at a time)	$50/hr	
Year-long tech curriculum help	$100	
Consulting/seminars/webinars	Call or email for prices	
	Total	

Fill out this form (prices subject to change).

Email Zeke.rowe@structuredlearning.net.

Pay via Paypal, Amazon, TPT, pre-approved school district PO.

Questions? Contact Zeke Rowe.

Structured Learning
Premier Provider of Technology Teaching Books to the Education Community